JOHN KELLOGG'S BOOK OF DOG TRAINING

Every dog, from the finest of purebred champions to the most exotic of mixtures, can become his owner's best friend—but not until he has learned a few basic rules of behavior. Teaching your dog to obey is not always a simple task, but in this authoritative and easy-to-follow guide, John Kellogg shows that it can be an enjoyable and rewarding one for both you and your pet. For many years a successful trainer and teacher of obedience training, the author believes that any dog can be taught to obey, and he has developed a consistent and effective program that requires no more of an owner than some common sense, patience, a love of his dog, and a few minutes a day. Beginning with the usual puppy problems of house training, riding in cars, and jumping up, Mr. Kellogg gives step-by-step instructions for teaching your dog to adjust to family life. Once your dog has learned to respect the tone of your voice, it is only a short step to more complicated commands and before long he will have graduated from the novice class to advanced utility training. Although this book is designed for the average family that may want nothing more than a few good manners from the canine member of the household, programs for the expert are included as well, together with the 1970 revised Obedience Regulations of the American Kennel Club for those who are interested in showing.

With drawings by G E O R G E F O R D

John Kellogg's Book of Dog Training

1976 EDITION

Published by
Melvin Powers
WILSHIRE BOOK COMPANY
12015 Sherman Road
No. Hollywood, California 91605
Telephone: (213) 875-1711

Library of Congress catalog card number: 74-119779
Printed in U.S.A.

Acknowledgment
The American Kennel Club: "Obedience Regulations,"
Copyright 1952, 1963, 1964, 1968, 1969
by The American Kennel Club. Reprinted by permission.

Reprinted by permission of The Viking Press, Inc.

Printed by
HAL LEIGHTON PRINTING CO.
P.O. Box 1231
Beverly Hills, California 90213
Telephone: (213) 983-1105

ISBN 0-87980-028-3

"The biggest dog has been a pup."
—Joaquin Miller (1841–1919)

"The best thing about this book is that when he was writing it or reading what he had written, the author had only one hand to use on the leash and training collar. I recommend that all dogs get it for their people."

—Tyndrum Lilias, Mr. Kellogg's West Highland White Terrier

CONTENTS

PREFACE

My interest in dogs and dog training began when I was six years old. It was then that my family acquired a German shepherd, who became devoted to me, and I decided I was going to teach him to pull my express wagon. I got myself a long pole to the end of which I tied a piece of meat. Then I harnessed the dog to my wagon and held the meat in front of his nose. In less than no time he had wrapped the wagon and me around a telephone pole. He got the meat, and I learned that dog training was more complicated than I had bargained for. When the dog died, my family and I were so upset, that a friend of ours gave us a smooth-haired fox terrier. It took the terrier only a short time to win the love and affection of the whole family, and he became my constant companion and pal.

My mother often tells of coming home to find the family

laundry tubs and towels out on the front lawn with a sign that proclaimed DOG WASHING, 5 CENTS. Fortunately for my mother's linen, the business was never very successful. As I grew older, and a paper route became my first true business venture, the terrier and I became a common sight in the neighborhood. By the time he died, I had made a vow never to be without a dog. I bought my next puppy, a cocker spaniel, with money I had earned delivering those papers.

The years passed until I entered the Coast Guard in 1942. By 1943 the Coast Guard had opened a dog-training school. Hearing of this, I immediately applied and was transferred to this division. Upon completion of the basic dog-training program, I assisted in the installation of trained dogs at beach points along the East Coast. At the close of the war, I supervised the feeding, general care, and maintenance of the dogs waiting to be sent home. During all this time, however, I had extensive instruction in the care, handling, and training of dogs; and, incidentally, acquired a wealth of experience in handling men.

It was back at my first training center that a ninety-pound German shepherd by the name of Chico was assigned to me. He and I went through the war together, but we were separated when Chico received his discharge papers from the Canine Unit and went to live with my parents. Once trained to attack a man's right arm and work swiftly up to his throat, the "civilian" Chico was perfectly content playing with my small nephews.

My family, at first reluctant to accept a large dog during wartime, was soon so happy to have him that various members gave up their meat ration points for weeks at a time so Chico could have his daily pound of hamburger.

On my return home the local paper reported: "It was a happy reunion when these two old friends met two weeks ago, even though Chico could only bark out a happy 'Woof' when he saw his master and trainer."

The First Kollege of Kanine Knowledge

After my discharge in the spring of 1946, feeling that I had developed a simple and unique method of teaching people how to train their dogs, I organized a class in show obedience for the kennel club in my home town. In September of 1946 I moved to the Philadelphia area, where I organized and opened to the public the Kellogg Kollege of Kanine Knowledge. In these classes the owner brings the dog to school and trains him under my instruction.

During the past twenty years I have coped with all types of dogs . . . and all kinds of people. One woman brought her Pekinese to class one night but kept him on her lap. When I asked her to put him on the floor she said, "Oh, no . . . my dog's feet never touch a public floor. He will learn from watching." He must have been a very clever dog. Neither he nor his mistress ever returned to class.

The lessons that I have developed over the years are detailed in the pages that follow. They are intended for, and can prove most valuable to, the family that owns and loves its dog, whether the animal be purebred or mixed, male or female. This book is also for the owner who wants to help his dog become a better citizen, fun to live with and obedient without being sullen; and for the owner who is interested in showing his dog in obedience classes. Many of the commands, exercises, and performances are based on the regulations of the organization that sets the standards for the obedience trials. I am, therefore, grateful to The American Kennel Club for its permission to include the latest revised version of its regulations, dated December 1, 1969, which appears in the Appendix beginning on page 91.

I would also like to call attention here to The Fund for Animals, Inc. The purpose of this group is to prevent misuse and abuse of our many animal friends by giving assistance to existing societies and by establishing new agencies, where necessary, throughout the world. Any interested reader can write to the fund at: 1 Wall Street, New York, New York 10005.

In a more personal vein, I am particularly grateful to Miss Sarah Mortimer, a dear friend, whose encouragement helped me carry forward my work with our canine friends. I also want to thank Mr. Gary Bub for his assistance and moral support. And last but not least, thanks go to my wife, Charlotte.

CHAPTER 1

Owning a Dog

Why Do You Want a Dog?

Is it because your neighbor owns one, or because your child, husband, or wife wants one? Perhaps a neighbor or a friend just had a new litter of puppies arrive at his house and you could not resist taking one home. Or perhaps you were out riding one Sunday afternoon and stopped at a roadside kennel "just to look." The resistance you might have had up until then melted away, and one of the little darlings is now yours. What a pity! Did you stop to consider what you had taken upon yourself and your family: the job of raising and caring for the puppy throughout his life?

Before a living creature is taken into a home, everyone in the family should be aware of what is in store for him— the duties that are expected and the inconveniences that will surely occur. A dog that is not part of the family can become

| 3

a real problem in the home. A little dog without proper training can get an entire family "into his hands" within a few months. It might be well to remember that many people cannot live with their grown children, let alone an adopted dog. The chances of finding a compatible dog are about the same as those of finding a compatible mate.

So if you are prepared to accept a dog in the house—not leave him tied outside—let us understand a few things before we proceed with the training lessons.

What You Can Expect When You Have a Dog

EXPECT: Dog hair on the furniture, rugs, and clothing.
To take the dog outside morning, noon, and night, fair weather and foul.
Some of your friends to be annoyed with the dog.
Your neighbors to be annoyed because of his barking or running.
To be inconvenienced because you might have to leave a very nice party in order to feed him.
To spend extra money for food and veterinarian bills.
Accidents on rugs and floors.
The puppy to chew on things such as shoes, hats, rugs, socks, and anything else that might be lying around.
The puppy to jump up on people.

With proper training, most of the above can be corrected; you and your dog can and will be true and happy friends.

Companion or Attacker? Friend or Foe?

People have dogs for the most astounding reasons. The kinds of dogs they have are even more amazing. I have any number of calls from people who have acquired German shepherds or dogs of that type because they want a protection or guard dog. A German shepherd or a German-shepherd type, however, doesn't guarantee a good protection dog. People bring dogs to me and show me wonderful pedigrees while the animals are cowering under a chair or behind their owners. A dog must have a particular kind of temperament or disposition before he can be trained to be a protection dog. Most people today fail to realize that it takes careful selection by qualified experts to find a dog suitable for this particular work. Consider the aggressive dog that snarls and snaps the minute anyone, sometimes even the owner, gets close to him. People may feel he would make a good dog for guard work, but they are wrong. I would much rather train an even-tempered, mild-mannered dog, if he is qualified, for guard work than have a snarling, snappy, sharp animal on the leash or running loose on the property.

Many people also fail to realize the effect a sharp dog can have on the whole family, even though he may never bite anyone. If you happen to have young children, in all probability the dog is friendly with them, or you certainly would not keep him. But you must consider your children's friends and playmates: they may not come over to visit after your dog has snarled and snapped at them once or twice. Nine times out of ten the family that owns such a dog has to dispose of him before he is three years old. Let's keep the dog as a full-time member of the family.

A Dog Is a Family Responsibility . . . Especially for Children!

Many parents find that their children benefit enormously from owning a dog. If a child is shy or not quite as talented in some things as a brother or sister, the sense of accomplishment that comes from training a dog well may help him develop self-confidence. Consider also the exceptional child who is bored with the usual games and sports. Even if he shows no interest whatsoever in participating in them, he might find a healthy outlet in training his dog.

A dog should not, however, be left to the mercy of a young child; parents must be prepared to exercise proper supervision over the dog's care and training. A young child is not ready to begin caring for or training a dog until he knows the difference between right and wrong. A puppy is not a toy to give a child and then forget about, nor is he a device to teach a child responsibility. Just as it is unfair to expect a dog to suffer tail-pulling, kicking, and other forms of abuse, so it is unreasonable to neglect him because Billy forgot to feed or water him on schedule. The dog should be cared for by every member of the family as the need arises, and he should be let out or walked by anyone in the house who sees that the dog needs to go out. How would you like it if you had to go to the bathroom but couldn't until a certain member of the family said it was all right? This is not family living, which is what you want to create.

Caring for Your Dog

Since this book is a guide to training rather than a manual of dog care, I won't discuss feeding, grooming, breeding, and so forth, in any detail; but I hope that the following general remarks will anticipate some of the questions you may have as you begin to think about your dog's education. There are a number of good books available on the subject of dog care, and I would suggest that you obtain one of these for reference. Your most important source of information, however, is the veterinarian, who should be at your disposal for regular treatment as well as emergencies. Consider the choice of your dog's doctor as carefully as you would the choice of your family physician, since he is the key to your dog's health and well being. Make yourself familiar with the licensing and dog laws in your area and be sure to obey them.

Feeding

If you are inexperienced and have a dog that is a problem eater, talk with your veterinarian and take his advice. I *would* like to point out, however, that many dogs can and do live on all sorts of strange diets. I once knew a woman who claimed that her dachshund would eat only hot dogs and ice cream with whipped cream. The fact that the dog was six years old and appeared healthy and happy could not be denied, but I believe this was an exception. I think that if I had quizzed her more extensively, I would have found that the dog also had bits of meat and a few dog biscuits daily.

The fun in owning a dog is that he is a companion and friend, so let's treat him as such. Make the preparation of his food as simple and easy as possible. My experience has been that if you have a healthy dog or puppy, and can start him on a well-balanced prepared-food diet, do just that. We travel with our dogs a great deal, so I try to select a brand of food that is available in most parts of the country. Once I have selected a diet for our dogs, I try never to change it. Consequently we have always had healthy dogs and never a problem eater.

On today's market there are hundreds of prepared dog foods. Many of the manufacturers have spent hundreds of thousands of dollars on research as to what is best for a dog. But you must remember that *you get what you pay for*. Many people will buy bargain foods and then complain that the dog won't eat, is too skinny, or sheds too much. Your dog's diet can have a significant influence on the condition of his coat. Feeding your dog can be as vast a subject as feeding your family, and the amount of time and trouble you want to expend is up to you.

Puppies Will Eat Anything!

If you have a very young puppy in the home, do not leave matchbooks, pins and needles, or staples lying around. Many things are stapled today; and if the staples get on the floor, a puppy can get hold of one and injure himself seriously. Watch out for certain toys. Every puppy or dog should have a plaything, but be careful what you give him. I suggest rawhide rather than rubber toys, and will always remember the following incident. Some friends left two basset hounds with me while they went to Europe. The dogs were two years old, and my friends insisted that the dogs had always had rubber toys with bells in them and had never once chewed them up. The owners had been gone less than three weeks when I realized that one of the dogs wasn't acting quite right. I took him to the veterinarian, who, after a lengthy operation, presented me with the end of a rubber bone that he had removed from the dog's intestine. Luckily the dog's life was saved, but the owners had a veterinarian bill of over one hundred dollars. This could happen to any of us if we are not careful about the type of toy we buy for our pet.

What about Breeding the Family Dog?

The household that breeds its dog without giving serious thought to the problems that arise usually makes a mistake. There should be far more consideration given to bringing a living creature into the world than the fact that your friend or neighbor has a cute dog which you think would make a nice mate for your family pet. I certainly would never deny the fact that it is an educational experience for your children; but it also can lead to heartaches, financial problems, and general strain on the whole household. If you have prepared yourself and your family by reading the available books and discussing the subject with your veterinarian, if you have prepared yourself to remain tied to your home for three or four months, if you have prepared a place for the puppies to be born, and an area for the puppies to play in outdoors as well as inside, everything will probably work out satisfactorily.

Puppies, Anyone?

Then there is the problem of disposing of the puppies. I have learned through experience, and I think most breeders would agree, that when you give a dog away, you are asking for more trouble and problems than if you sell the dog even for a nominal sum. But I would like to warn would-be breeders that even the selling of purebred puppies is not as simple as most people believe. You should use as much discretion and thought in placing a puppy in a home as the new owner should use in selecting him. For example, I once knew a family that had a litter of Great Dane puppies. They sold one of the puppies to a pleasant-looking family with a young son. A few weeks later, the breeder stopped by to see how the puppy was getting along. He found him sitting on the greasy garage floor alongside a skimpy piece of dirty newspaper. The wife insisted on keeping the puppy there because she couldn't take the chance of his dirtying the rugs. But she and her husband were very pleased with their son's behavior. He had only stepped on the dog's paws a few times. The lady of the house was unembarrassed, and apparently this was standard operating dog care in her household. "I am so glad we got a big dog this time," she confided happily. "Our last dog was too small. My little boy kicked it down the cellar stairs and broke its back." After hearing this gruesome bit of family history, the breeder refunded the purchase price and took the puppy home with him. In this case, the dog was rescued in time, but some pets aren't so fortunate and must remain with their owners. The only expression of unhappiness open to them takes the form of rebellion. They may sulk, refuse to listen, attack other dogs, forget their house training. When life really gets to be too much for them, they are apt to run away.

Spaying

Many people have asked me whether a dog's temperament or ability to learn is affected by spaying or castration. I have never found this to be the case, and believe that no harm will be done as long as the owner is absolutely sure he does not want to breed his dog or show him in breed shows. As far as obedience training is concerned, a dog that has been altered is still eligible for showing if he is otherwise qualified.

CHAPTER 2

Beginning Steps

First Things First

Formal obedience training is not usually begun until a puppy is about six months old, since most dogs do not coordinate well before that age. But there are several things you can start to teach him from the very day he is brought into your home: one is housebreaking (see page 18); another is his name. When you select a name, be sure to choose one that is easy to pronounce and that doesn't sound like something else. For example, we know a puppy who was named Moe. Every time he committed an indiscretion he would be reprimanded with "No!" which sounded like his name and led to a great deal of confusion. I have also known Great Danes called Pussy Cat, Peachie-Cheechie Pie, and other similar inappropriate names which, like bad jokes, soon wore

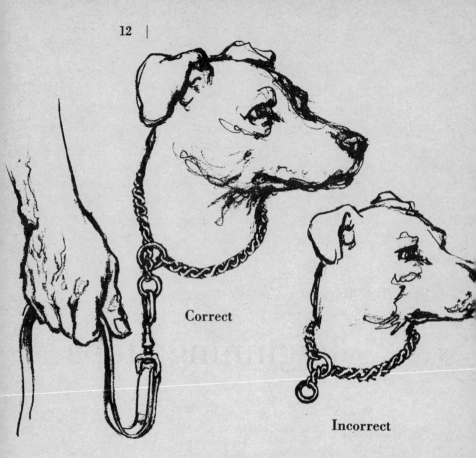

Correct

Incorrect

thin but not before the dogs had become accustomed to them. If your puppy is purebred, you might select a derivative of his registered name.

While he is getting used to his name, you can begin to teach him the routine of housebreaking, but there are some preliminary rules and routines that you should be teaching yourself at the same time.

Equipment

The only equipment you will need to start training your dog is a five- or six-foot leather leash and a chain training collar. The leash should have a strong bolt-type snap. There are two ways to put a collar on a dog, but only one is correct for obedience training. Be sure to study the illustration. If you don't put the collar on correctly, you will not get the proper action from it when handling your dog on the leash. It is important to attend to these details early, since every exercise in this book should be started On Leash.

Concerning the leash, keep in mind these two important "don'ts": don't let your dog chew on it or use it as a toy; don't ever strike him with it. Remember that the hand that praises should be the hand that punishes. Accordingly, if you are forced to spank your dog, use your hand and not a newspaper. Punishment of any kind, if necessary, should never be overdone or dragged out. Simply get it over with quickly and go on from there. Repeated or extensive punishment is pointless, since your dog will have forgotten the reasons for it, and you run the risk of breaking his spirit or making him nasty.

Keep Lessons Brief

Like human beings, dogs vary in their capacity to learn. By careful observation you can soon determine whether your dog is alert, attentive, and quick to learn or whether he is easily distracted, naturally scatterbrained, or simply uninterested. As soon as you know what you can expect of him, pace your instructions according to his demonstrated ability to understand. Although training will not change his basic temperament and intelligence, his disposition and behavior are directly influenced by proper care and handling, which will bring out the best in him, just as good manners bring out the best in people. But training does not happen accidentally or automatically; and it is the degree of your effort, patience, and understanding that will affect the speed of his progress.

In any case, do not make the lessons too long. Two daily

half-hour sessions or four fifteen-minute sessions are more effective than one hour-long lesson. Dogs, too, can get restless or impatient or tired, and you don't want your dog to lose interest or develop resistance to you by forcing him beyond the limits of his endurance. Consistency and frequent practice are far more important than the duration of each lesson. I recommend that you devote a full week to teaching your dog each new command, incorporating into every lesson a review of the commands you have already taught him. Don't try to cram too much into your dog's mind at once. Be thorough, not hasty, and don't expect too much of him too soon. Enthusiasm and praise from you will make each session enjoyable for you both, and your consistency, firmness, and patience will encourage his respect and willingness to learn.

Use Time Efficiently

The way in which you use the time spent in practice with your dog is as important as the amount of time you spend. Train yourself to use a minimum of movements and short commands so that your dog will understand what you want of him without hesitation or confusion. You want him to respect and obey you, so maintain absolute authority at all times. Remember that *how* you teach him, not *what* you teach him, is the key to success. Many owners who have become discouraged in training their dogs do not realize that the real reason for their lack of success is usually their own ineffectiveness rather than the dog's inability to learn.

Basic Obedience Training

Generally speaking, every dog—large or small, purebred or mixed, male or female—can be trained to some degree. If your dog is shy and timid, a great deal of praise and encouragement will help. Although it will be necessary to force him to do some things against his will, the dog will show remarkable improvement if you do not baby him too much. On the other hand, if you should own a forward and intense dog, you must be very firm with him. Your commands must be definite, and you should not give him too much praise. And if he is just plain stubborn, you must urge him constantly. Be severe and demanding; but when he obeys, praise him well.

One of the most important principles of training is the use of both physical and verbal commands at the same time. This principle is applied to corrections and praise. A well-trained dog is admired not only for what he can do but for the fact that his trainer can get him to obey by using either his voice or a simple gesture. This is not difficult to achieve if you employ both methods from the very beginning. In using your voice remember that dogs don't understand words, only sounds; so the proper tone is essential. Even if you are consistent with the words you use, their meaning will be lost on your dog if you aren't consistent with the pitch and inflection of your voice. At the same time, your movements should be efficient and authoritative whether you are giving a command, making a correction, or giving him praise for a job well done. Learn to coordinate your voice with your movements and make a habit of using the same words and gestures each time you work with your dog.

Making Corrections

When you first begin teaching your dog, he will have no idea of what you want him to do. Therefore a certain amount of force and correction of mistakes is necessary. By trial and error and repetition he will gradually learn to perform each exercise on command, without leash or collar pressure.

You must always make it a point to keep your dog on your left side during the training process, with the leash carried in your right hand. The leash should be doubled up but not wrapped around your hand, and the lead should be short but not tight. Allow enough slack for the dog to make a mistake and for you to correct him, but don't allow room for excessive freedom, or you will have no control. The timing of your corrections is very important. Do not let him get away with

The snap correction
should be sharp but brief

errors or misbehavior. A delayed correction has no effect, so be sure to correct him immediately and let him know you mean it.

To be more specific, as soon as your dog makes a mistake, apply sharp pressure to his collar by a positive snapping motion on the leash. Do not be hesitant about snapping him in the right direction. This way he will soon get the idea that a sharp tug on the neck means that he must do what *you* want him to do, not what *he* wants. The larger the dog, the more force you will have to apply. Don't be afraid to use both hands on the leash if necessary. But don't drag the dog along or keep the collar under constant tension. Apply pressure, then release it immediately. You do not want to punish your dog unnecessarily, since he will have no idea at first what he has done wrong. After he has learned what it is you want him to do, correction should not be necessary unless he forgets and makes a mistake, at which point a quick snap of the leash is enough to remind him.

A Word of Praise

Of equal importance as correction to your dog is ample praise for performing properly and behaving well. Once again use your voice and mean it. Put genuine feeling into the words "That's a good boy!" or "You're doing fine!" Use any words you like, but be sure you speak in a pleasant tone that makes him look up at you and wag his tail. Remember, enthusiasm is contagious. Your dog will quickly learn right from wrong, without confusion, through a "bad" experience (snap on the leash) or a "good" one (praise).

At the end of each lesson, after your dog has performed to your satisfaction, release him with the cheerful command "Okay" to let him know he may move freely on the leash. Don't let him confuse "Okay" with praise or become excited.

A word of praise

Now that you have learned some of the basic principles, it is time to start teaching your pup what he must learn in order to become a full-time member of the family. Here are some ways of coping with classic puppy problems.

Winning the War of the Puddle

The tension and trouble stemming from housebreaking have often broken strong men and resolute women, ultimately quashing additional training efforts. There are two ways of approaching the problem and both require time and patience. First, I have found that the best way to housebreak a puppy is to begin by taking him outside On Leash on his first day in the house right after you have given him as much water as he will drink. If he performs, praise him. Thereafter take him to the same spot the first thing in the morning and immediately after every meal. I stress On Leash because you will then have some control over his activities. The secret is to curb his desire for play and to practice patience until he does what he is there to do. Then praise him lavishly. Second, should you want to break your dog to paper first, this is a method that I have used successfully. Choose one room for the housebreaking chamber. It should be convenient to a door leading outside. Spread newspaper over the entire floor. Put his bed in the same room, as far from the door as possible. Normally, he will go as far away from his bed as he can, so you can gradually reduce the newspaper until it covers only the area nearest the door. When you see him head for that area, snap on his leash and take him outside to accomplish his purpose. He must not be rushed; it is essential that you let him take his time. When he completes the function outside, praise him so that he will know he has pleased you.

Dogs are creatures of habit, so be sure to take him On Leash to the same place every time you take him out.

Car Riding

Many people have complained that their dogs will not ride in the car properly. The best way to prevent this problem is to teach your puppy to ride quietly in the back seat. I do not approve of dogs riding in the front where they can interfere with the driver or get down on the floor under a pedal and perhaps cause a serious accident.

Before you let your dog get into the car, make him sit and wait while you open the door. Then say "Okay, you may get in." Do the same thing when you get him out of the car. You may have to ask somebody to get into the back seat with him to make him sit quietly while you open the door. Let him remain sitting quietly for a minute or two and then say "Okay, you may get out." Use the word "Okay" as a command to let your dog know he may move freely on his leash. Use it cheerfully, but don't let him confuse it with praise or become excited.

Don't try this lesson on the busiest street in town. Try it in your own driveway where you can take the time to go through the procedure once or twice a day. Make a regular training session out of it. If you have acquired an older dog who is in the habit of getting very excited in the car, you can train him to sit quietly, by sitting with him in the back seat and using the leash and your voice to make correction if he misbehaves.

Jumping Up

One way to prevent this problem is to refrain from exciting your puppy or encouraging him to greet you enthusiastically when you come into the house. If he is already in the habit of jumping up, I find it best to take a forward step and bring a knee sharply against his chest. This won't harm him, so don't offer sympathy when he falls over. If he is a small dog and kneeing is difficult, step lightly on his back feet—just enough to cause him discomfort.

A larger dog may need even more drastic treatment than mere kneeing or stepping on his hind feet. When he jumps on you (your family and friends should practice this method also), hold his front paws in your hands while you lift your knee into his chest. As impact occurs, release his paws and let him drop to the floor with the command "Off!"

Some jumpers choose the door or a piece of furniture for their target, and this can be destructive as well as annoying. If you are in the house at the time the dog is jumping on the

Correcting the jumping-up habit

door to get out, it may be possible to sneak up behind him and slap him on the rump with the command "Off!" This correction is the most efficient, but you will find it is only possible to accomplish this once or twice. He will soon be leary of committing this error in your presence, and there is no assurance that he will not do it as soon as you leave him alone. If he does continue, lock the dog in the room or house and, instead of leaving, stand outside and wait until he makes the error of scratching on the door or jumping on the furniture. Then go back in, put the leash on the dog, and make your correction: snap the leash as you say "Off, bad dog!" A few minutes each day devoted to this discipline eventually should convince the dog of his errors. If you start these corrective measures early, you will prevent a jumping problem that could last throughout your dog's life.

Obedience Is Fun

All dogs can become better citizens through obedience training, but keep in mind the fact that no dog can be trained if the methods are haphazard or inconsistent. A specific plan like the common-sense program outlined in this book, close attention to details, and above all the patience to proceed one exercise at a time will eventually win out. Once you are committed to a training routine, you will find that the work is not arduous and that the results more than repay the effort expended. Your dog will learn to respect and obey you—and enjoy doing so—when you act with authority and praise him when he has done well. Most dogs love to demonstrate what they have learned when they know it pleases their owners, and they will soak up new instructions quickly and accurately as the training progresses.

Your dog is one of a kind, so adapt the training to the individual rather than to the breed. A good pedigree is no guarantee of good temperament or keen intelligence; it is your understanding of your dog's good qualities and your ability to develop them that will result in a responsive, compatible companion of whom you can be proud. And remember, your consideration for his health and nourishment, plus plenty of affection, will contribute as much to molding his overall character as will good training.

CHAPTER 3

The Basic Commands

Now that you and your dog have established a friendly and effective working relationship, we can proceed to the basic commands you are going to teach him. Whenever I use the name Rex, you should substitute the name of your own dog. I suggest that you first read each lesson through at least once so that you will have an idea of what is to come. If you are not sure what is meant, read the lesson over again before trying it with your dog.

Sit

The first of the basic commands is "Sit!" You will use it to teach your dog to sit quietly at your left side. His leash will be gathered loosely in your right hand. This may seem awk-

"Rex, Sit!"

ward at first, but after a little practice you will find you have more control and will be able to use your left hand to better advantage with the dog and leash in this position.

First, make sure the collar is on properly, and put your dog On Leash. Next, gather the leash in your right hand, leaving the left hand free. Then grasp the leash near the collar with your left hand and take hold of the collar with your right hand, which is still holding the gathered leash.

Release the leash from the left hand and tighten the collar with the right hand by pulling up on it. At the same time, press down on the dog's rump with the left hand. As you tighten the collar and press down on the dog's rump, give a firm command: "Rex, Sit!" Using this procedure, it should be possible to force the dog to sit straight at your left side. As soon as the dog sits, release the collar from the right hand, but still hold the gathered leash there.

The dog in the
Sit position

Remember this rule: When you take the leash with the *left* hand, you must take the collar with the *right*. The most frequent mistake a new trainer will make is to grab the leash with the left hand and try to snap the dog to a sitting position, failing to take the collar with the right hand so that the left hand can be used to guide the dog to a straight Sit. Let the leash remain loose enough for the dog to try to do *wrong* so that you can show him what is right, but do not give him enough leash to allow him excessive freedom of movement.

If your dog stays in the Sit position, then praise him with "That's a good boy!" or "Good puppy!" Stand straight yourself. The dog's feet should be pointed in the same direction as yours. If he should move—and at first he probably will—repeat the procedure. If he should jump on you, use the left hand low on the leash and the right hand on the collar to snap him down with the correction "No! Bad dog!" Then repeat the procedure and the command "Rex, Sit!"

Do not permit your dog to get into the habit of leaning against your left leg. If he does, take a little side step to the right. If he slides to the floor, grasp the leash low with the left hand and the collar with the right, snap him back to the Sit position, and repeat the command "Rex, Sit!" You should not say "Rex, Sit down!" Get into the habit of using one-word commands.

If your dog tends to assume an awkward sitting position, you should correct him before he assumes the full Sit position. He will soon get the idea of what you are trying to teach him. These corrections must be done in such a manner that the dog is not frightened. If your corrections are too severe, the dog will shy away from you, so a happy medium must be found.

Once you have mastered the technique of making your dog Sit command again. Take one step forward, make your dog sit straight, then praise him. But take the time to insist that he do it right each and every time. Consistency is of utmost importance in teaching any command. Your dog wants to please you, but you must be patient in teaching him what will please you most.

Heel

Once you have mastered the technique of making your dog Sit, you should proceed promptly to teach the second basic command, which is "Heel!" This command is used to tell the dog to come to your left side, whether you want him to sit or walk.

First, sit the dog on your left side with his head up close to your knee, the leash gathered loosely in your right hand and your left hand free. Now step forward on your left foot. Give the leash a brisk snap with the left hand and at the same time in a firm voice give the command "Rex, Heel!" It is important to keep the dog's attention and to give the leash a hard snap and then let go. Do not pull or tug on the leash, or use a long, exaggerated motion. The leash should tighten only momentarily, and one good snap is worth a series of snaps. Obviously your dog can never walk correctly at your side if he is dragged along instead of being snapped back into place, or if the leash is constantly kept tight. It is the snap on the leash and the command of your voice that will make the difference in whether you succeed in teaching your dog to Heel or not.

If the dog responds and remains at your left side in Heel position, praise him with "That's a good boy!" or "You're doing fine!" If the dog goes too far forward, do not try to keep up with him; slow up and snap the leash with the left hand, using a backward motion, and repeat the command "Rex, Heel!" If he persists in going ahead of you, turn in the opposite direction and snap the leash once more, using both hands and repeating the command "Rex, Heel!" Should the

Heeling On Leash

dog lag behind, snap the leash and urge him to hurry up while you speed up your own pace. He will soon realize he is more comfortable at your side.

But remember the rule: Always keep the leash slack when walking the dog, and keep your left hand off the leash unless you are making a correction. Every time you snap the leash, be sure to give the command "Rex, Heel!" Every time you give the command "Rex, Heel!" be sure you snap the leash.

In other words, the command and the snap on the leash should be given together.

In practicing the Heel command, stop and start frequently. Always start on the left foot. You will be surprised how soon this will mean something to the dog. Each time you start, give him the command "Rex, Heel!" Walk along and make a right turn. Then make a left turn. Now make an about turn to the right, away from the dog. If he starts to make a mistake, take this opportunity to show him what is right, to convince him that you are serious about his training. Remember, he learns right from wrong through a good or bad experience. Therefore watch your dog at all times, so you can anticipate his wrong moves and correct him immediately.

Each time you stop, make the dog Sit at your side with the command "Rex, Sit!" The Heel and Sit commands should be practiced in conjunction with each other.

Later on, when your dog has mastered the Heel and Sit commands at home, take him out of your yard and away from the house. Practice in shopping centers or on busy streets, but always On Leash. Stop at every corner and make him Sit before you cross the street. Train him to Heel and Sit around other dogs and strange people, as well as around members of your family.

Figure Eight

Now is the time to teach your dog the Figure Eight exercise. Its purpose is to help train your dog to obey you on command without turning his attention elsewhere. At the same time, it will help to consolidate the training you have already given him to Sit and Heel.

For this exercise you will need the help of two people standing quietly about eight feet apart and facing each other. They are not to acknowledge any attention your dog may try

Figure Eight Exercise

to give to them. If people are not available, you may use two chairs positioned the same distance apart, with the seats facing toward the center. Should you use chairs, place a dog biscuit or some other favorite food morsel on the edge of each one to tempt your dog.

Start this lesson in the center, between the two people or chairs, with your dog sitting at your left side in the Heel position. Now give the command "Rex, Heel!" and walk around each person or chair. When you have completed a full Figure Eight around the chairs, stop in the center and give the command "Rex, Sit!" Repeat this procedure several times.

Next, perform the same exercise, but stop in the center each time you go around a person or chair. Remember to start off on your left foot with the command "Rex, Heel!" and to give the command "Rex, Sit!" each time you stop. Keep at it until your dog will go around in a Figure Eight without sniffing at the people or the food, and without drawing away from your side. You must encourage your dog with lots of praise if he stays at your side and keeps up with you. If he should pull away or lag behind, be sure to give a sharp snap on the leash, using both hands and the command "Rex, Heel!"

Continue to give the command "Rex, Heel!" each time you start. However, your dog should eventually come to a straight Sit by your side whenever you stop, without your having to give him the command to Sit.

Sit, Stay

The next basic command is "Stay-y-y!" It is used whenever and wherever you want the dog to remain in the same position for any length of time. Once again you will use a one-word command. You must never use the dog's name when you want him to stay behind; and when you leave him you must always step out on the right foot.

The command is just plain "Stay-y-y!" No more, no less. You should never say "Now you stay there!" or "Please stay there; I'll be right back!" Remember, you are *commanding* him, not *asking* him; so be firm, and mean "Stay-y-y!"

To teach this command, first Sit the dog at your left side, with the leash hanging loosely in your right hand. Now, with

a.

Sit, Stay Exercise

c.

b.

the palm of your left hand in front of your dog's nose, give the command "Stay-y-y!" Do not touch the dog's nose. Walk directly away from him, starting on your right foot, until you are at the end of the leash. Turn around and face the dog, and switch the leash to your left hand. Hold your right hand at your side, palm open and facing the dog. Do not say another word to the dog or repeat the command.

If the dog does Stay for a moment or two, return to him by going around his left side to your original position; but be sure to keep the leash on the right side of the dog, away from his body. Gather up the leash into your right hand and wait a second or two, standing still to his right. Then praise him with "That's a good boy!" or "You're just great!" Please notice that I said wait a second or two before you praise

Stand, Stay Exercise

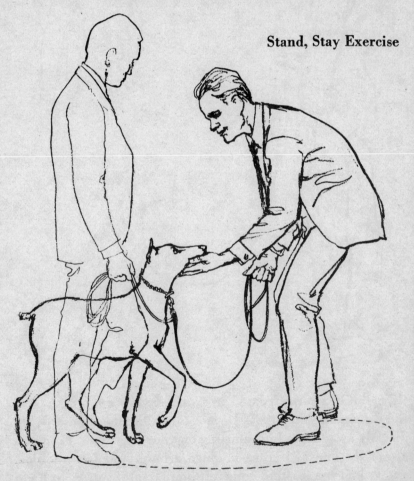

him. If you praise him too soon, he is going to get excited and move before you get all the way back to his right side.

If the dog has moved, lain down, or come with you, go directly back to the Heel position, without going around him, and snap the leash sharply, saying "No, no, bad dog!" Then repeat the exercise and the command "Stay-y-y!" Never run back to the dog or get excited or lose your temper. If you do, stop and relax. Then take a deep breath and start all over. Remember, this is an exercise in control for both you and your dog. As when he was learning to Sit, you can expect your dog to move at first. Don't be discouraged. Instead maintain the attitude that you have told him to "Stay-y-y!" and, there-fore, you expect him to do just that. But if he should move, be prepared to make a firm correction.

Gradually extend the time you stay away from the dog to as much as five minutes. Then tie a piece of rope or line to the end of the leash and move even farther away—perhaps around the corner or into another room. Now have other members of the family or a friend walk around the dog so that he will become used to motion without moving himself. If he Stays until you return to the Heel position, be sure to give him lots of praise. Should he move, make a prompt and firm correction. Practice every day and exercise patience with this lesson. You will be surprised how soon you will get results.

Stand, Stay

The next basic command, "Stand, Stay!" is used to instruct the dog to stand still in one spot while you leave him, and to remain standing there until you return. If you have trained your dog to Sit and Stay correctly, you will have very little trouble with the Stand, Stay exercise.

To teach this command, start with the dog sitting at the Heel position. Then with the command "Rex, Heel!" start forward on your left foot, with the leash gathered in your right hand and the left hand off the leash. While the dog is walking, reach down with the left hand and place it under the dog's neck. Keep walking and give the command "Stand, Stay!" as you walk away from the dog. After a couple of steps, turn and face the dog. If he stays there, back away to the end of the leash. Switch the leash to your left hand, and hold the palm of your right hand at your side, facing the dog. If he should move or sit down, go directly back to the Heel position *without* going around the dog, snap the leash, say "Phooey!" or "Bad dog!" and try again. Once he remains standing and stays, even if just for a moment, return directly to the Heel position by walking *around* the dog's left side with the leash in your left hand, keeping the leash on the right side of the dog, away from his body. The dog should remain standing after you have returned to the Heel position and until you take one step forward and give him the command "Rex, Sit!" Then praise the dog with "That's a good boy!" or "Good Rex!" As in teaching the Sit, Stay, gradually extend the time you leave him, and have someone move about him or stroke his back so that he will learn not to be distracted.

The important thing to remember is that the dog must be Heeling on a loose leash, and that you should keep moving ahead of him after you give the command "Stand, Stay!" Remember, too, that you do *not* use his name when you want him to remain behind.

If you have mastered the Stand, Stay exercise On Leash and your dog remains in that position while someone has moved up to him and stroked his head and back, you are ready to take off his leash and try to have him Stand and Stay Off Leash. In order to do this correctly, have your dog at the Heel position, remove his leash, and give it to someone. Then with the command "Rex, Heel!" move out with your dog and proceed as you did On Leash. When the dog is in the Stand position, say the command "Stay!" and swing your left palm

in front of his nose. (It is no longer necessary to touch the
dog's neck with your left hand.) Walk at least six feet beyond
him, turn around, and stand facing him. Then have someone
approach the dog from the front and touch his head, body,
and hindquarters. After this has been accomplished, return
to your dog, walking around his left side to the Heel position.
The dog should remain standing without moving his feet or
body after you have returned to the Heel position. It is important that you wait a few seconds after you have returned before you give the dog the command to Sit. (I usually count
silently to fifteen or twenty.) Then take one step forward and
give him the command "Rex, Sit!" Praise the dog as before.

Down

The basic command on which we will work next can be a
little bit difficult, so I am going to ask you to pay very close
attention. You are going to teach your dog to lie down. This
command is done very slowly and precisely. You must show
no excitement. Neither should you struggle physically with
the dog in your attempt to make him obey.

To begin, Sit your dog at the Heel position, with his leash
in your right hand and your left hand free. Now take hold
of the dog's collar under his neck with your left hand and pull
down. At the same time bend your left arm so that the forearm is over the dog's back, between his shoulder blades. If
the dog should stand up at this time, stop what you are doing
and make him Sit. If he remains sitting, continue with the
lesson. Carefully drop the leash from your right hand. Place
the palm of your right hand in front of the dog's nose and
give the command "Rex, Down!" As your right hand passes
the dog's nose keep firm pressure on his back with your left
forearm. Try this several times. If the dog does not lie down,
it may be necessary for you to pull his forelegs slowly out in

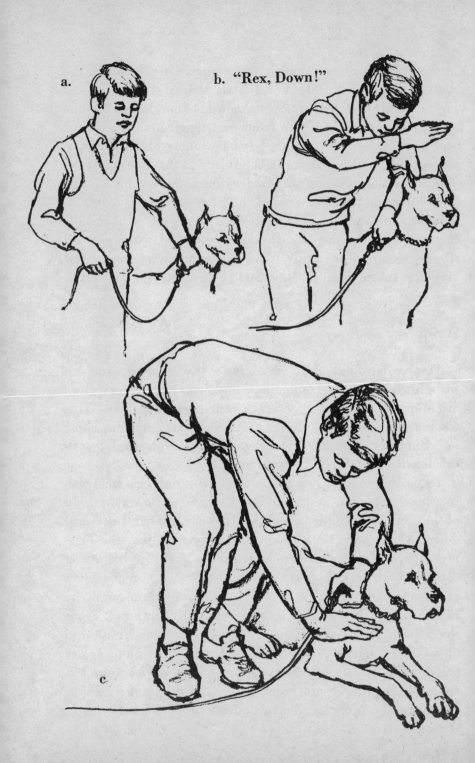

a.

b. "Rex, Down!"

c

front of him with your right hand after you have given the signal to Down. As soon as he is down, stand up straight. Take the leash in your right hand, keeping it loose. If the dog gets up, say "No," and then repeat the exercise exactly as before. Don't just push him down or try to hold him down. You must teach him, without wrestling, that you want him to lie down when you give him this command.

Once the dog is down and stays briefly, take hold of the leash with your left hand and snap him to a Sit position with the command "Rex, Sit!" Don't praise him when he is in the Down position. Wait until he Sits, and then give him lots of praise. Try the Down command a few times each day, but don't overdo it. Always hold onto the leash, and progressively lengthen the time he stays down.

Once your dog has learned to stay down for an appreciable length of time, reach down with your left hand and give him the command to Stay, just as you did in the Sit, Stay command, and go to the end of the leash. See that he remains down and in the same position. Have other people go over to him to see if he will move or be otherwise distracted. If he should get up, return directly to him. Remember, do *not* go around him, but correct him and repeat the command. If he stays down, return to him, being sure to walk around his left side, keeping the leash on his right. He should remain down until you give the command "Rex, Sit!" Then praise him with "That's a good boy!"

Come

The last of the basic commands is probably the most important one. It is the command "Come!" To teach a dog to come to you depends a great deal on how much the dog respects your voice. If you have trained him to do all the other basic commands, you should have very little trouble in teaching him this one.

Begin with the dog sitting at the Heel position and the leash loose in your right hand. Give him the command to Stay, and go to the end of the leash. Face the dog and stand with your feet slightly apart. Now, with a firm but pleasant voice that he would be able to hear from a distance, give the command "Rex, Come!" Snap the leash at the same moment, and gather it up in your right hand as he begins to approach you. Praise him all the while, and tell him what a good boy he is. Make sure he comes directly to you, the faster the better. Then make him Sit directly in front of you. You may have to bend down and make him Sit straight.

Once he is sitting straight directly in front of you, count mentally and slowly to at least five. Now take hold of the leash down near the collar with your left hand. Keeping your right foot in position, move your left foot back and give the command "Rex, Heel!" At the same time swing the dog counterclockwise into the Heel position, and bring your left foot even with your right foot again. Then praise and pet him, and tell him how pleased you are: "That's a good boy!" A great deal of praise is very important with this lesson.

In teaching your dog this exercise, be sure to alternate it with Staying the dog and returning to him. Otherwise he may begin to think that you always want him to Come when you leave him, instead of only on command.

Once your dog is Coming to you, Sitting straight in front of you, and coming around to Heel on the command, lengthen the leash and try it from a greater distance. Be sure not to tangle the leash or scare the dog with it.

When you are sure your dog will Come to you On Leash from a Sit position every time you give him the command "Rex, Come!" you may then give him the command "Okay!" and let him be free on the leash to sniff, walk about, or do as he wants. When he thinks he is free, again give him the command "Rex, Come!" Make him Sit in front of you and Heel. Then give him lots of praise: "That's a good boy!" How easy this will be if you use your voice enthusiastically.

a. "Rex, Come!"

b.

c. "Rex, Heel!" d.

Heel Off Leash

If your dog is on a loose leash, Heeling close to you and making right and left turns, changing pace with you, and Sitting straight at the Heel position each time you stop, now is the time to take him Off Leash. When your dog is Off Leash, only two facts are going to keep him at your side: you have trained him properly with your voice and actions; and he has learned to respect you. First, do the basic commands

Heeling Off Leash

On Leash. When he is Sitting at the Heel position again, take the leash off and fold it in half. Carry it in the right hand, making sure the snap is in the palm of your hand. The dog, seeing the leash, will be reminded to stay at your side. When you start out on the left foot, be sure to use the same tone and command that you do when he is On Leash. At the same time use a sharp forward motion with the left hand. If he forges ahead, do not panic. Instead, give him the command "Rex, Heel!" Keep walking forward. If he bolts, slap your left hand with the leash to alert him. Then bring him back to the Heel position with the command "Rex, Heel!" Do not show nervousness. Handle your dog with the same confidence you had when he was On Leash. Be sure to keep up a line of chatter when he is first Off Leash. Remember, your voice will keep him at your side. Let him know you trust him. If your dog is walking too wide too often, reach down and snap the leash on him. Then give him a snap back with the command "Rex, Heel!"

Try the Figure Eight exercise making sure he does not lag or crowd you. Be prepared to meet the errors with the proper corrections. When you start Heeling your dog Off Leash, do not make the session too long. A very few minutes each day is best, and then lengthen the time Off Leash gradually. If he makes a mistake, put him back On Leash and make a firm correction.

As soon as he has learned to Heel Off Leash, try some of the other commands you have already taught him. Before long you should be able to make him Come to you by using the command "Rex, Come!" while keeping your arms at your sides. You may also teach your dog to Come on signal without the verbal command. After you have taken him Off Leash, swing your right arm across your chest in an upward motion as you say "Rex, Come!" When he becomes familiar with the gesture, he will Come to you as readily as he does when you use the verbal command alone. Don't use the gesture every time you say "Rex, Come!" He should learn to respond to both signal and command even when they are used separately.

Review

Now for a little review—a sort of practice test for the student dog. Your assistant should give you the commands as we state them here and test and score you as a judge might in the obedience ring at a dog show. If you want to try this according to The American Kennel Club regulations, your ring should be thirty-five by fifty feet for indoor trials and forty by about fifty feet for outdoor ones.

Our review commands will be as follows: FORWARD, HALT, RIGHT TURN, LEFT TURN, ABOUT TURN, SLOW, NORMAL, FAST. These directions may be given in any order and may be repeated. The principal feature of this exercise is the ability of the dog to work with his handler as a team. When your assistant gives you the command FORWARD, you give the command "Rex, Heel!" and start walking. When he says HALT, you stop, and the dog should Sit automatically. Follow the rest of the instructions accordingly. Ready?

FORWARD ("Rex, Heel!") . . . HALT.

The dog should now be sitting at the Heel position, his feet pointing the same way as yours, the leash gathered loosely in your right hand.

FORWARD . . . ABOUT TURN . . . LEFT TURN . . . RIGHT TURN . . . HALT.

FORWARD . . . ABOUT TURN . . . SLOW . . . NORMAL . . . HALT.

FORWARD . . . ABOUT TURN . . . FAST . . . NORMAL . . . HALT.

EXERCISE FINISHED.

Now is the time to pet and praise your dog.

If you are eager to show off your dog's mastery of these basic exercises, you should be familiar with some of the commands that a judge will use in the ring.

FIGURE EIGHT. Try this exercise by using two assistants standing about eight feet apart. Start your dog at the Heel position between the two assistants. At the command FORWARD, walk your dog through in a full figure-eight pattern twice. There will be at least one HALT during the exercise and another HALT at the end.

STAND FOR EXAMINATION. When the judge gives the order PREPARE YOUR DOG FOR THE STAND EXAMINATION, stand or pose your dog, giving him the command or signal to Stay. Walk forward about six feet in front of him and turn to face him. The judge will approach the dog from the front and touch his head, body, and hindquarters. He will then step away from the dog and give the order BACK TO YOUR DOG, whereupon you walk around behind your dog to the Heel position. The dog must remain in the Stand position until the judge says EXERCISE FINISHED, and must show no shyness or resentment during the examination.

HEEL FREE. When this command is given, your dog is sitting at the Heel position. Remove his leash and place it outside the ring on a table and repeat the exercises that were given in the Heeling On Leash examination.

RECALL. At this order, you should sit your dog in the Heel position. When the judge says LEAVE YOUR DOG, give him the command or signal to Stay in the Sit position. You then move to the other end of the ring—a distance of about forty feet. When the judge gives the order to call your dog, call him with one command, "Rex, Come!" The dog should Come immediately and Sit directly in front of you. Upon orders from the judge to FINISH, move the dog smartly to the Heel position.

LONG SIT. Start your dog at the Heel position. Upon the

Judge's order to LEAVE YOUR DOG, give the command or signal to Stay, go to the opposite side of the ring, and face your dog. After one minute the Judge should give you the command BACK TO YOUR DOG. (In advanced classes the period will be three minutes.) Return promptly to your dog, walking around and behind him to your place in the Heel position. Your dog should not move from a sitting position until the Judge says EXERCISE FINISHED.

LONG DOWN. The Long Down is done in the same manner as the Long Sit with the exception that, on orders from the judge, your dog lies down and stays in a Down position for three minutes. (In advanced classes the period will be for five minutes.)

Well, how did your dog do? Perfect? Congratulations! But if he did make a few mistakes, don't be disheartened. Don't stop training him now. You are already well on the way to success with his obedience training, but you must continue to practice with him. Keep working with him regularly and frequently. Don't give up.

If you have mastered the Basic Commands, you may want to progress into the more complicated ones.

Drop on Recall

a. "Down!"

b. "Sit!"

CHAPTER 4

Advanced Training

Drop on Recall

If you have taught your dog to Down at your side with the hand signals as described in our basic course, you should have little trouble teaching him to Down when you are some distance in front of him, or to obey the Drop on Recall command.

Once again put your dog back On Leash and move him to the Heel position. Stay your dog and go to the end of the leash. Face him with the leash in your left hand and your right hand at your side. Raise your right hand, palm down, over your head. Take a step forward and bring your right palm down in front of the dog's nose with the command "Down." If he doesn't obey the command, grasp the lead near the collar with your right hand and pull your dog down again with the command "Down." Then step back to the original position

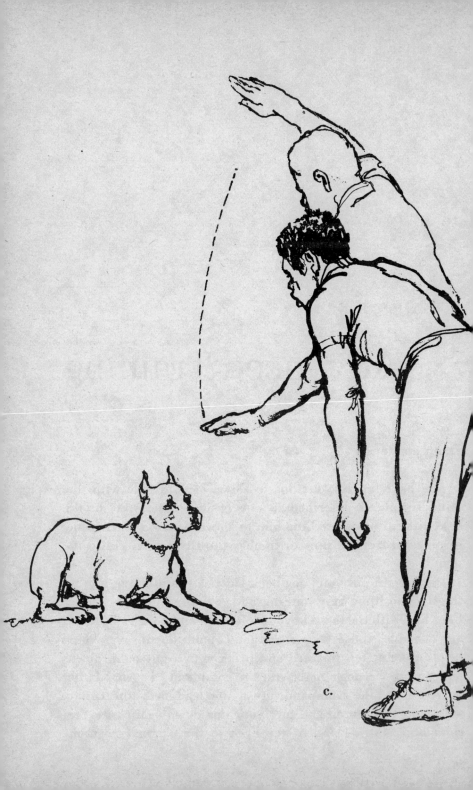

c.

in front of your dog leaving him Down. Count to five slowly. Now, in order to make him Sit, take a step directly in front of your dog. Raise your right hand, palm up, and give the command "Sit." If he doesn't obey immediately, put your right hand under the lead and snap your dog up to the Sit position with the command "Sit." Step back to the original position in front of your dog. Count to five again. Now walk around your dog to the Heel position. If he remains still, praise him: "That's a good boy! That's a good fellow!"

Repeat the exercise. After you have practiced it a few times, take the leash off your dog. Stay your dog, move out about five feet in front of him, and turn around. As you raise and lower your right palm, say "Down." You may have to take a step forward again for your dog to go down, or you may have to pull down on his collar. Step back from your dog. Wait a few moments, raise your right palm, and give him the command "Sit." He should move into a Sitting position without moving forward. Then call your dog as in the Recall. Have him Sit directly in front of you. Now with the command "Rex, Heel!" he should move around into Heel position. Again praise your dog: "That's a good boy!"

Once you have taught him this exercise Off Leash, put him back On Leash. Have your dog at the Heel position. With the command "Stay!" go to the end of the leash. Call your dog with the command "Rex, Come!" Run backward and, after a few feet, give the command "Down!" by raising and lowering the right hand as you speak. Your dog should drop to the floor. Leave him there making sure he is still one length of the leash in front of you. Give the command "Rex, Come!" Again he should get up, run to you, and Sit directly in front of you. Wait a moment. Then give him the command "Rex, Heel!" and praise him. Practice this On Leash. Then take the leash off and Stay your dog. Call your dog. When he is about halfway to you, give the command "Down!" by either moving your right hand *or* using your voice; in showing, you aren't allowed to combine both voice command and hand signal. If your dog drops to the floor, count silently to at least five and repeat the command "Rex, Come!" Once again he should run to you and Sit directly in front of you until you give him the command "Rex, Heel!" Then, as always after good work, praise him.

Retrieve on the Flat

Now let's teach your dog to carry the dumbbell. A wooden dumbbell is preferred, but a rolled-up newspaper thick enough to fit comfortably in his mouth may be used. You are going to teach him to hold it in his mouth and carry it. In working with the dumbbell make this a special treat for your dog. Start by showing the dumbbell to your dog. Let him smell it. Let him sniff it a bit. Wave it in the air. Excite him about it. "Do you want your dumbbell?" "Do you want your dumbbell?" When it is clear he is eager for it, make him earn the reward of working with it. Put the leash on your dog. Do a few of the basic commands, making him Heel and Sit. Once you have done this, make the dog Sit at the Heel position. Then take the dumbbell and offer it to him. If he does not take it immediately or if he resists taking it, drop your leash and pry his mouth open by exerting pressure with the thumb and first finger of your left hand against his lips. Do this gently but firmly, talking to him all the time you are exerting pressure. Tell him "Good boy." Use the words "Get it! Get it!" as you insert the object in his mouth. Then move your left hand under his chin to hold his mouth shut with as little pressure as possible. This becomes a delicate operation—the opening of his mouth, the inserting of the dumbbell, and the closing of his jaw around the object. Do not make him fearful as you say "Hold it! Hold it!" Eventually he will understand what you are trying to have him do. Some dogs will drop the object. If yours does, just pick it up and try again. If your dog holds the dumbbell for a second or two, place your hand on one end of the dumbbell as you continue to say "Hold it!" *He is not to release the object even though your hand is on it until you give him the command "Out!"* When you say "Out!" he is to release it into your hand. If he performs as he should on each command, give him plenty of praise. Pet him. He loves to hear you say "That's a good boy!" Never forget to praise. It is so very important. Continue to work on this dumbbell sequence. Hold it a few inches away from his mouth and try to make him reach for it. Some dogs may take quite a while before they will even hold it, but don't become discouraged. Muster up all your patience and continue to work on it. When your dog finally holds the dumbbell properly, we can proceed to teach him to walk beside you with the dumbbell in his mouth.

First, pick up your leash. Give the dumbbell to your dog with the command "Get it!" and then "Hold it!" Now give him the command "Rex, Heel!" With the dog On Leash, carrying the dumbbell, he must continue to hold the object as he Heels. If he Heels and Holds it, give him the praise he deserves. Now stop and make him Sit correctly at the Heel position. Reach down and take hold of the dumbbell. He should continue to hold it until you say "Out!" Then he should release the dumbbell into your hand; and you, in turn, should praise him.

Again, let me repeat that in all training with the dumbbell, you must be *sure* to make this a treat. Always make it something special he is allowed to do *after* he has Heeled, Sat, Stayed, and done other basic commands. You must remember to keep the dumbbell up on a shelf away from your dog. When you move over to get it down, this becomes his reward for doing his other exercises well.

Now that your dog can carry the dumbbell as he walks

beside you, our next move is to teach him to pick it up off the floor. To achieve this, have your dog On Leash at the Heel position. Once again excite him with the dumbbell a little bit. Wave it around and ask him if he wants his dumbbell. Now, with the dog On Leash, toss the dumbbell to the floor and say "Rex, Get it! Rex, Get it!" In all probability he will run over and pick it up. If he does not do this, lead him to the dumbbell and encourage him to pick it up. If he makes any move toward it, give him praise: "Good boy! Let's get the dumbbell! Let's get the dumbbell! Good boy! Rex, Get it! That's good!" Once he picks it up, have him come directly back to you by giving the command "Come!" Do not let him come to your side. He is to Come and Sit directly in front of you holding the dumbbell. If he does this, reach down and take hold of the dumbbell and give the command "Out!" He is to release the dumbbell. You do not want him to drop it into your hand or onto the floor. If he does, show it to him and say "No, bad dog!" Say "Rex, Get it!" If he picks it up and holds it, you say "Hold it! Hold it!" It is important that you make him wait before releasing it until you give the command "Out!"

After you have taught your dog to hold the dumbbell, to carry it, and to retrieve it from the floor, then increase the distance you throw the dumbbell as your dog responds. Have him On Leash. Say "Rex, Get it!" and go with him. If he picks it up, you run backward. Have him Sit directly in front of you while he holds the dumbbell until you say "Out!" Then give him the command "Rex, Heel!" and he should move around into the Heel position. Don't let him simply run back and Sit at your heel with the dumbbell in his mouth. Make him Sit straight, directly in front of you. Similarly when you throw the dumbbell out in front of him, do not let him run out to retrieve it the second you throw. Have him Stay. He must *wait* until you give the command "Rex, Get it!" Then he is to rush out, pick up the dumbbell, come

**Retrieving on the
Flat Off Leash**

a. "Rex, Get it!"

b. "Come!"

c. "Out!"

back, and Sit directly in front of you with the dumbbell in
his mouth. You grasp the dumbbell with your hand and say
"Out!" He gives up the object and continues to Sit in front
of you until you give him the command "Rex, Heel!" Once
he is at the Heel position, you praise him enthusiastically:
"That's a good boy! That's a good fellow! You're doing fine!"

Now let's take your dog Off Leash. Have him Sit straight and quietly at the Heel position, and try the entire procedure again. Praise your dog when he completes the Retrieve on the Flat. Then put the dumbbell back on the shelf for a while and go on to the next exercise. This first one will be to teach your dog to jump the High Jump.

Retrieve over High Jump

According to The American Kennel Club Obedience Regulations (see Appendix), the side posts of the High Jump should be four feet high; the jump should be five feet wide, and constructed to provide adjustment for each two inches of height from eight to thirty-six inches. It is suggested that the jump have a bottom board eight inches wide, including the space from the bottom of the board to the ground or floor, together with three other eight-inch boards, one four-inch board, and one two-inch board. The jump should be painted a flat white.

Occasionally you will hear someone say, "I don't want my dog to learn to jump. We have a fence around our home, and I am afraid he'll jump over it." If your dog has been taught all the other basic commands and you now teach him to jump *only* when commanded to do so, and at no other time, you should have no trouble. We shall proceed on the theory that your dog is a well-mannered, well-behaved animal whom we will now teach to jump on command.

First, have your dog sitting On Leash at the Heel position. The jump should be set no more than eight inches high to start. No matter what the size of your dog may be, whether he is a toy poodle or a Great Dane, start with just an eight-inch-high jump. Have your dog Heel with you up to the jump. Now let him sniff and smell it. Then take him back and have him Sit at the Heel position in front of the jump. Once again

**Learning to Retrieve
over High Jump**

a. "Over!"

walk up to the jump with him. Now say "Over!" as he steps
or jumps over. *You go over* using your left leg as a guide
for your dog. If he is a small dog, you may have to lift him a
little, using your left hand on the leash as you step over the
jump. But be sure to give him the command "Over!" Do this
a number of times, and soon you will find that your dog will
go over the first jump with enthusiasm. Once he realizes he

is to jump, you walk *around* the jump instead of over it with him.

Next, raise the jump a little higher. Perhaps to ten or twelve inches. Follow the same procedure at that height with your dog On Leash. He should be able to jump one and a half times his own height at the withers, from a minimum of eight inches to a maximum height of thirty-six inches. If your dog is

b. "Get it!"

eight inches at the withers—that is, eight inches from floor to shoulder—then he should be able to jump eight inches with no trouble. Continue to practice until your dog can jump the required height. Make it fun going over the jump, but do *not* allow him to become wild or overexcited. He must jump when you say "Over!" and *only* when you say "Over!" If you have any question about the height your dog should jump, see Chapter 2, Section 18 of the appendix.

Now let's take the dumbbell down from the shelf and put the two exercises together. Lower the jump so that your dog can see the dumbbell on the other side. Tell him to "Stay!" and throw the dumbbell over the jump. Tell him to "Get it!" He is still On Leash, so loosen the lead. As he goes forward, say "Rex, Over! Get it!" The dog should then take the jump and pick up the dumbbell. Make him return to you over the jump by giving the leash a slight tug and the command "Rex, Over!" as he comes back over the jump. Remember that he must take the jump in both directions. Many dogs fail in obedience trials because they do not return over the jump.

When he returns, he should Sit directly in front of you with the dumbbell in his mouth. He is not to release it until you reach down to take the dumbbell and say "Out!" Let him Sit straight, directly in front of you for about ten seconds. Then give the command "Rex, Heel!" Each time he does this properly, give him lots of praise.

Repeat this exercise a number of times On Leash. Then take him Off Leash. Make the dog Sit beside you at a reasonable distance from the jump. Hold the dumbbell in your hand. Give your dog the Stay command. Throw the dumbbell over the jump. Give the command "Rex, Over! Get it!" He should go over the jump, pick up the dumbbell, and return over the jump. If he tries to go around the jump on the way back, block his path with your body. Force him to return *over*

Retrieve
over High Jump

the jump and Sit directly in front of you with the dumbbell in
his mouth. Once again reach down and have him release the
dumbbell on the command "Out!" Stand up straight, count
ten to yourself, then give the command "Rex, Heel!" Now
praise him: "That's a good boy! That's a good fellow!" Never
forget the praise.

If he does not perform correctly, you must respond with
"No, bad dog!" Put him back On Leash and repeat the

exercise. Be sure to show him where he is wrong and to make the proper corrections if he does not perform exactly as ordered.

Broad Jump

Let's proceed to the Broad Jump, an interesting exercise and one you should have little trouble with if you have taught your dog to jump the High Jump correctly.

Notice that there are four separate hurdles that can be telescoped for convenience. Make the boards eight inches wide with the largest measuring about five feet in length and six inches high at the highest point. The hurdles should be painted a flat white and arranged in order of size, with the low side of each hurdle and the lowest hurdle facing the dog. They should be evenly spaced out to cover a distance equal to twice the height of the High Jump set for your dog: four hurdles are used for a jump of 52 to 72 inches; three hurdles for a jump of 32 to 48 inches; and two hurdles for a jump of 24 to 28 inches.

When attempting this exercise, you should stand with your dog sitting at the Heel position ten feet in front of the jump. No matter what the size of your dog is, start with just a single hurdle and with your dog On Leash. Walk up to the hurdle and, as you approach it, say "Rex, Jump!" As before, you may have to use your left hand on the leash to help your dog over the first hurdle. Do this several times until the dog jumps normally over the hurdle at the command "Rex, Jump!" Then increase the number of hurdles until the desired length is reached. Each time you approach the hurdle go over it yourself, or at least go around the side, as you say "Rex, Jump!" If he refuses to jump the hurdles, turn the first hurdle on edge. This should encourage him to jump over instead of stepping on the hurdle.

After some practice with your dog On Leash, try taking him Off Leash. Make him Heel as you go up to the hurdles. Then say "Rex, Jump!" and see if he won't hurdle the distance required. When your dog has mastered this, Sit your dog ten feet in front of the hurdles and give him the command "Stay!" Go up to the right side of the hurdles, facing the right side of them with your toes about two feet from the jump, anywhere between the first and last hurdles, as in the illustration. Command your dog, "Rex, Jump!" As he jumps the

Broad Jump

a. "Rex, Jump!"

b.

c. "Rex, Heel!"

hurdles, make a right-angle turn while the dog is in mid-air so that you will be facing him when he returns, comes up, and Sits directly in front of you until you give the command "Rex, Heel!" and he moves into the Heel position. Praise him and let him know he's done a good job. Eventually your dog should be able to jump the Broad Jump without touching it and without any secondary command or signal from you, and return to the Sitting position immediately in front of you.

Review

Before you start, have the High Jump and the Broad Jump set up properly. Remove your dog's leash. We will begin the review with the same exercise we did in the basic review, except that the dog will be Off Leash. As before, when your assistant gives the command FORWARD, you say "Rex, Heel!" You should not speak, praise, or give another command to him until your assistant says EXERCISE FINISHED. When the command HALT is given during the exercise, your dog should Sit automatically at your side without a command. Follow the rest of your assistant's commands accordingly. Ready?

> FORWARD . . . HALT.
> FORWARD . . . ABOUT TURN . . . SLOW . . . NORMAL . . .
> ABOUT TURN . . . HALT.
> FORWARD . . . FAST . . . NORMAL . . . ABOUT TURN . . .
> HALT.
> FORWARD . . . LEFT TURN . . . RIGHT TURN . . . ABOUT
> TURN . . . HALT.
> EXERCISE FINISHED.

Now, do the Figure Eight as described in the basic review but do it Off Leash.

Drop on Recall

Have your dog Sit in the Heel position Off Leash. Give him the command "Stay!" When your assistant gives the command LEAVE YOUR DOG, walk about twenty feet and turn to face the dog. When the command CALL YOUR DOG is given, you say "Rex, Come!" When he gets about halfway to you, give him the command "Down!" Leave him Down until your assistant gives you the second command to call your dog. The dog is to Come and Sit directly in front of you until the command to finish is given. Do not praise him until your assistant says EXERCISE FINISHED. Then give him all the praise he deserves. Ready?

> ("Stay!")
> LEAVE YOUR DOG.
> CALL YOUR DOG. ("Rex, Come! Down!")
> CALL YOUR DOG. ("Rex, Come!")
> FINISH. ("Rex, Heel!")
> EXERCISE FINISHED.

Retrieve on the Flat

Start with your dog in the Heel position. As before, you can tell him to Stay before your assistant's command to throw the dumbbell. On the command TAKE IT reach down and, saying "Out!" take the dumbbell from the dog's mouth. Stand up straight while the dog remains sitting directly in front of you.

> ("Stay!")
> THROW IT . . . SEND YOUR DOG. ("Rex, Get it!")
> TAKE IT. ("Out!")
> FINISH. ("Rex, Heel!")
> EXERCISE FINISHED.

Retrieve over High Jump

> ("Stay!")
> THROW IT . . . SEND YOUR DOG. ("Rex, Over!")
> TAKE IT. ("Out!")
> FINISH. ("Rex, Heel!")
> EXERCISE FINISHED.

Broad Jump

> ("Stay!")
> LEAVE YOUR DOG . . . SEND YOUR DOG. ("Rex, Jump!")
> FINISH. ("Rex, Heel!")
> EXERCISE FINISHED.

Now try the Long Sit, which is executed at dog shows in the same manner as given in the basic review except that you should be away from your dog and out of sight for three minutes. The Long Down is also executed in exactly the same way as in the basic review, but you stay away and out of sight for five minutes.

Well? How did your dog do? Perfect? Congratulations! Once again, keep working with your dog regularly and frequently so that he will be a real pal and companion rather than just another dog. You could have no finer reward for your efforts.

CHAPTER 5

Utility Training

Although the material and exercises that follow can help you train your dog for show obedience competition in the Utility class, our prime interest is to make you and your dog more compatible. At this point you can teach him two or more exercises at the same time, rather than proceeding one by one. In other words you may be training your dog for Scent Discrimination and teaching him the Signal exercises in the same lesson period.

If you have watched Utility work in the obedience ring, you may feel that it is terribly difficult. It could be if you ever try to do it without the basic exercises. But if you take it as just another step in training your dog to be a companion, it will follow with very little trouble. If you have given your dog both the basic obedience and the advanced training, Utility training should not be difficult for him to learn.

Scent Discrimination

You will need ten articles similar in size to your dumbbell, five of metal and five of leather (see Appendix, p. 121). They must be identical in appearance and numbered for identification. You should also have a pair of tongs with which the articles can be picked up, so that whoever is handling the articles (other than you) does not leave his scent on them. If you are handy, you can make the articles yourself. If not, you can purchase them from your pet supply dealer. The size you use depends upon the size of your dog.

Begin by giving your dog one of the leather articles to hold, and let him carry it in Heel position. Then make him Sit beside you. You toss and he'll retrieve as we did in the advanced training course. When he retrieves the article well, go through the same exercise with the metal article. You may have some difficulty at first with the metal object because many dogs do not like to pick up metal. Once he has retrieved these articles in sight, hide a different article each time in the exercise area, in the grass, or behind a piece of furniture. Try to get him to find it by using his nose. If he cannot find it, go out with him and point to the article and say "Find it!" Once you feel he knows what he is looking for and that he is to retrieve the article and bring it to you no matter where it may be, then you should begin to use an article board or carpet.

Cut a three-foot square of wood or carpet (I prefer the carpet because you can sew right into it). Mix and scatter four of the metal and four of the leather articles about six inches apart, and fasten them on this field. Air the wood or carpet for a day or two in order to remove your scent. (Better yet, have someone else make the carpet for you, so that your scent is less likely to be on the articles.) Rub each of the two remaining articles in your hands until your scent is thoroughly absorbed into them; you want your dog to differentiate between the articles thrown and the articles already attached to the board or carpet. It is important that you do this each and every time just before you throw an article and that you let your dog sniff the palm of your hand just before he leaves your side.

Place the carpet or board some distance from you and throw the leather article out near the board where the other articles are placed. Then send your dog after it. It doesn't matter if he goes near the carpet as long as he picks up the article with your scent on it and brings it back to you. Make him Sit in front of you, then take the article from him and praise him. Lots of praise! Talk to him all the time he is working to give him the confidence he needs.

If he should start to pick up the wrong article, give him a gentle reprimand such as "No, no, bad dog!" Make him feel that you are helping him, although he is doing it on his own. You have to be very careful at this point that the dog doesn't become frightened of the articles and hesitate to pick up the proper one.

As soon as he has learned to retrieve the article thrown near the carpet, make him Sit and Stay while you place the article directly on the carpet or the board. Be very careful not to touch any of the other articles. If you do get your scent on anything but the one loose article, take a day or two off to air the carpet with the articles tied to it. As I said before, it is a great help if you can have somebody else handle the carpet.

When you send your dog, he may try to pick up one of the articles stitched to the carpet. Correct him with a very quiet firm "No, Find it, Find it." Once he finds the right article and brings it back to you, praise him generously. I would suggest that you use the leather article each time until your dog has learned this part. Then switch to the metal one. Your dog is trying to please you, so praise him when he does well. Remember, Scent Discrimination training will take some time, so be patient with your dog.

Learning Scent Discrimination

a.

b.

Scent
Discrimination

a.

b.

Once he is picking up the articles and bringing them to you each time, it is time to have help. After you put your scent on an article, have your assistant carry it to the carpet using tongs, being careful not to get his scent on the article, and place it while you and your dog have your backs to the articles. Then turn the dog around and send him. If he makes a mistake, don't be discouraged and don't discourage your dog.

As soon as your dog retrieves the proper article, he should return to you briskly and Sit directly in front of you holding the article until you reach down and give the command "Out!" Then you stand up straight and give your dog the command "Heel!" Turn around, and have your assistant take the other article and repeat the exercise until the dog has retrieved both articles that have your scent.

Once you have trained your dog to use his nose in retrieving the first two articles, it is time to loosen one or two more from the carpet as long as he brings back the right article each time. Continue to loosen the articles until it is possible to place them about fifteen feet away from you and work them in this fashion. When your dog has used his nose each time to select the correct article, he has completed the Scent Discrimination exercise.

Directed Retrieve

I must assume at this point that your dog can do the earlier exercises proficiently. Therefore a simple explanation of the Directed Retrieve should suffice. Just remember to start slowly and not to expect too much too soon. You will need three short white work gloves. Take each glove one at a time and let your dog carry it and become familiar with it. This should not take long. Then place one glove a short distance from him and send him to retrieve it, just as he did the dumbbell on

Directed Retrieve

the flat. When he has done this a number of times, put two gloves about fifteen or twenty feet apart and train him to retrieve the one you indicate. Pivot your body toward the glove you want him to retrieve and point with your left hand as you say "Get it!" If the dog does not respond by moving to the correct glove, go with him to the glove, pointing and encouraging him with the words "Get it!" Try it again until the dog picks up the glove on the signal alone. Alternate right and left gloves as you practice. When he is doing this perfectly, put the third glove between the two on the ground and practice the exercise until he can retrieve any of the three you indicate.

As the dog approaches you with a glove in his mouth, he should Sit directly in front of you and continue to hold the glove until you reach down and give the command "Out!" at which time he will release the glove to you. Standing up straight, give him the command "Heel!" Once this exercise is perfected, he has completed the Directed Retrieve.

Signal Exercises

Teaching your dog to work with hand signals alone is very impressive and can be great fun, since it appears to be much more difficult than it actually is.

If you have followed my instructions from the very beginning, every movement you make means something to your dog. If, when you started out, you were careful to use the palm of your left hand and your left leg in a forward motion when you started Heeling the dog Off Leash, the dog should be conditioned by now to move with you when you make this gesture.

If, when you trained your dog to Stand and Stay, you used the palm of your left hand in front of his nose with the command, your dog should be conditioned to Stand with a hand motion and Stay.

If you taught your dog to lie down when you raised your right hand sharply and lowered it slowly, your dog should be conditioned to Down with that motion.

Signal Exercises

a. Stay   b. Down   c. Sit

If you taught your dog, using your right palm toward him in an upward swing, to Sit from a Down position, your dog should be conditioned to Sit with that motion.

If, in teaching your dog to Come, you swung your right hand across in front of your chest, your dog should be conditioned to Come with that motion.

d. Come

e. Heel

f. Exercise Finished

The Signal exercises are nothing more than putting these fundamental movements to work for you and your dog without voice commands. So let us now go through the exercise that is required in the Utility class at dog shows. Whether you show your dog or use the exercise to impress your friends, this routine brings you and your dog one step closer to perfection. When you first start teaching your dog the Signal exercises, there will be times when it will be necessary to use your voice, but try to keep this to a minimum.

Start with your dog at the Heel position Off Leash. Move your left foot forward and swing your left hand, palm outward, in a forward motion. Briskly Heel your dog in a straight line. When you stop, your dog should automatically Sit at your side without any further signal from you. Start forward again with your dog at your side, make a right or a left turn and, after a distance, make an about turn. At this point, swing your palm toward the dog's nose, as in the Stand, Stay exercise. This time you want your dog to stop and remain standing. You continue to walk forward leaving your dog behind. After fifteen or twenty feet, turn around and face your dog. He should remain standing. This time raise your right hand sharply above your head and lower it slowly. If you have taught your dog to Down from in front properly, he should drop into a Down position. Let him remain in the Down position while you mentally count to five or six very slowly. Then swing your right arm, palm upward, over your head; and your dog should move to a Sit position without coming toward you. Once again count to five or six as you lower your arm to your side. Call your dog to you by swinging your right arm across in front of your body. With this movement your dog should come running and Sit directly in front of you. Now swing your left arm counterclockwise, and your dog should snap around to the Heel position at your left side.

At this point, your dog should be in the habit of watching your movements. If not, it is up to you to go back to the former exercises included in the basic and advanced commands in order to refresh yourself as well as your dog, so that he will pay attention to your arm and body movements.

Directed Jumping

Since you have already taught your dog to jump the High Jump (see page 56), the Bar Jump will not pose much of a problem. You will need a five-foot bar with a diameter of two to two and a half inches, painted in alternating three-inch sections of black and white. Although you will eventually need two four-foot upright posts to support the bar, you may start by attaching it to the top of the High Jump you have been using. Simply drive a nail into each upright about one inch above the top board your dog has been jumping. The next step is to train your dog to jump the bar with the solid High Jump boards in place. Put the dog back On Leash and walk him up close to the jump so that he will see what he is to jump over. Then take him to the jump by running beside him with the leash in your right hand. As you get to the jump give him the command "Over!" If your dog knocks the bar off at first, it may scare him a little; but reassure him and continue practicing On Leash until he gets used to going over the bar. As soon as he will jump the Bar Jump Off Leash, you should start to eliminate the High Jump boards by removing them one at a time, starting at the top. In this way the dog will get used to going over the Bar Jump as the open space between the bar and the boards becomes greater. By the time you have removed the last board, your dog should be taking the jump without touching the bar or trying to run under it.

The next step is to train your dog to jump over either the High or Bar Jump on command. Place both jumps in the middle of the ring so they are about twenty feet apart, set at right angles to the sides of the ring. Command your dog to take one or the other jump Off Leash while you run along beside him. Do not run around the ring taking both jumps in the same round; return to the starting place each time you complete a jump.

The next step is to teach the dog to "Go out." Once again begin this On Leash. Run with the dog the full length of the fifty-foot ring, saying "Go out!" or "Away!" (The exact words are not terribly important, but "Go out!" seems to be the usual command.) Run in a straight line, moving your right hand as you run, pushing the palm outward as you say the command. It does not matter whether the dog Heels at this point as long as he manages to keep up with you. When you get to the fifty-foot mark or the end of the ring, stop and back up slightly, saying "Come, Sit!" so that he turns around and Sits directly in front of you. After you praise him, return him to the Heel position and walk nonchalantly back to the starting point. It is important that he Heels as you return.

Repeat the exercise over and over until the dog goes all the way out and turns and Sits at the end every time. Now take him Off Leash and give the command "Go out!" using your hand motion at the same time. If he doesn't run to the end on his own, put him back On Leash and repeat the original exercise. If he still seems confused the next time you try it without the leash, you might ask someone to stand at the end of the ring. The person should remain quiet, however, while you give all the commands.

If there is no one available to help you, you can use his rolled-up leash or a biscuit or other morsel. Run him out to the end of the ring and drop the leash or biscuit where you want him to Sit. Then take him back to the starting point and send him once again, using your arm with the command "Go out!" When he gets near the object give the command "Rex, Come, Sit." Some people use a dumbbell for this exercise, but I think you are apt to confuse the dog because he will probably try to pick the dumbbell up, thinking that you want him to retrieve it. I particularly do not like to see people use a pully, since they tend to tug on the dog's neck as he is going out, inadvertently punishing him for doing what they want him to do.

When the dog has learned that you want him to run alone to the end of the ring and to turn and Sit on the command "Rex, Come, Sit," you can drop the word "Come" and say only "Rex, Sit." Do not slur the words together. The name "Rex" is enough to attract his attention and turn him around, while "Sit" is the actual command.

Directed Jumping

The next step is to teach the dog to go over a jump as he returns to you. When the dog is out, walk over to one of the jumps and point to it as you say "Over!" As soon as he jumps over it, have him Sit directly in front of you. Then give him the command "Heel!" and praise him. Repeat the exercise, indicating the other jump. Continue to practice until it is only necessary for you to pivot and point to the jump you want him to take, instead of walking over to it. Do not let him return directly to you; always make him go over the jump.

Be sure to use lots of praise with this exercise, but wait until he is in the Heel position to do so. This is a difficult exercise for the dog, and it will take a great deal of patience and practice to perfect it.

Group Examination

This last exercise in the Utility class for dog shows is entitled "Group Examination." In this exercise the dog must Stand on command and remain standing, as you taught him in the basic commands, while someone touches his head, body, and hindquarters or examines him. The difference here, though, is that your dog must stand with other dogs on both sides of him while you are at a distance of thirty feet. The dog must remain standing for three minutes while a stranger (the judge) goes over him, opening his mouth to inspect his teeth, gently running a hand down his back, and pressing on his hindquarters. The dog should remain standing until *you* return and the judge gives you the command EXERCISE FIN-ISHED. This exercise can be easily accomplished by extending the length of time and distance that you remain away from your dog during the Stay exercise. You need nothing more than extensive practice and an assistant to examine the dog.

By this time you and your dog should be accomplished performers. You should work as a team, presenting a picture

Stand for Examination

of companionship and devotion that is acquired only through love, patience, hard work, and time.

Review

Now, for a review on your Utility work! In this review, as in the other sections, you will need someone to give you the commands aloud so that you can test yourself. Utility work is always performed without the leash at obedience trials, so let's try to go through this review while you work with your dog Off Leash. Follow the rest of the instructions accordingly.

Scent Discrimination

Ask your assistant to select one article from each of the two sets, using tongs so that he doesn't touch them with his hands. Have him put the two articles on a table or chair near you.

Turn yourself and your dog so you are facing away from your assistant while he picks up the rest of the articles in his hands and scatters them in a circle ten or fifteen feet away from you. You will then choose one of the two articles on the table, put your scent on it, and hand it back to your assistant. Using tongs, he will place it among the other articles on the ground, being careful not to touch them. When he says SEND YOUR DOG, you will lower your hand to the dog's nose and turn around, giving him the command "Find it!" Your dog should go briskly to the group of articles and find the one with your scent on it. There should be no penalty for a dog who takes a reasonable length of time examining the articles, provided he is working all the while. Your dog should then return smartly and Sit directly in front of you holding the article until your assistant gives you the command TAKE IT. You should then reach down and with the command "Out!" take the article from the dog. Stand up straight while the dog remains sitting directly in front of you. At the instruction FINISH, say "Rex, Heel!" and he should move around to the Heel position. Repeat the procedure for the other article.

SEND YOUR DOG. ("Find it!")
TAKE IT. ("Out!")
FINISH. ("Rex, Heel!")

Directed Retrieve

Your assistant will order you to stand with your dog Off Leash in the center of the ring between the High Jump and the Bar Jump. He will then place three white gloves—one at your right, one in the center, and one at your left—about three feet from the sides of the ring. When he says RIGHT or CENTER or LEFT, you must send your dog to the designated glove. The dog should retrieve the glove and return to you promptly and Sit in front of you until your assistant gives the command TAKE IT. Then you reach down and take the glove from your dog as you say "Out!" Stand up straight while the dog remains sitting. On the command FINISH, have him move around to the Heel position as before.

RIGHT. ("Rex, Get it!") . . . CENTER . . . LEFT.
TAKE IT. ("Out!")
FINISH. ("Rex, Heel!")

Signal Exercises

Your assistant should use the following commands. You, of course, say nothing to your dog but command him to perform using signals alone.

FORWARD . . . LEFT TURN . . . RIGHT TURN . . .
ABOUT TURN . . . HALT.
FORWARD . . . SLOW . . . NORMAL . . . ABOUT TURN
. . . FAST . . . NORMAL . . . HALT.
FORWARD . . . ABOUT TURN . . . STAND YOUR DOG
AND LEAVE YOUR DOG . . . DROP YOUR DOG . . .
SIT YOUR DOG . . . COME . . . FINISH.

Directed Jumping

When your assistant says SEND YOUR DOG, use the command "Go out!" Your dog should go to the far end of the ring at which time you say "Rex, Sit!" Your assistant will indicate which jump is to be taken, and you will command your dog by signaling the proper jump and saying "Over!" When he returns to you after jumping, he should sit quietly until the assistant says FINISH and you give him the command "Rex, Heel!"

Group Examination

When your assistant gives the command STAND YOUR DOG . . . LEAVE YOUR DOG, walk away from him. The dog must remain standing at least three minutes while the assistant examines him. When he says BACK TO YOUR DOG, return to your dog, who should remain standing until your assistant gives the order EXERCISE FINISHED, at which time your dog should return to you at the Heel position.

How did you and your dog do? Perfect again? Congratulations! By the time you reach this stage in the training, you will naturally be thinking about obedience showing, if you have not already begun to show your dog off to friends. If you are seriously interested in shows, it is a good idea to practice these exercises regularly in the presence of other dogs and their owners. Your dog will learn to disregard the distractions that might interfere with his performance, and the competition will be good for both of you. I am sure that your success so far has inspired some of your friends and neighbors to start training their own dogs, so company should not be hard to find.

In the appendix that follows, you will find the complete rules and regulations for obedience trials held under the auspices of The American Kennel Club. In addition to providing essential information for potential competitors, the rules will serve you as a useful guide in maintaining the high standards that you have achieved.

Good luck!

APPENDIX

Obedience Regulations of
The American Kennel Club, Inc.
Revised and effective as of December 1, 1969

Purpose

Obedience trials are a sport and all participants should be guided by the principles of good sportsmanship both in and outside of the ring. The purpose of obedience trials is to demonstrate the usefulness of the pure-bred dog as a companion of man, not merely the dog's ability to follow specified routines in the obedience ring. While all contestants in a class are required to perform the same exercises in substantially the same way so that the relative quality of the various performances may be compared and scored, the basic objective of obedience trials is to produce dogs that have been trained and conditioned always to behave in the home, in public places, and in the presence of other dogs in a manner that will reflect credit on the sport of obedience. The performances of dog and handler in the ring must be accurate and correct and must conform to the requirements of these regulations. However, it is also essential that the dog demonstrate willingness and enjoyment of its work, and smoothness and naturalness on the part of the handler are to be preferred to a performance based on military precision and peremptory commands.

CHAPTER 1

General Regulations

Section 1. *Obedience Clubs.* An obedience club that meets all the requirements of The American Kennel Club and wishes to hold an Obedience Trial at which qualifying scores toward an obedience title may be awarded must make application to The American Kennel Club on the form provided for permission to hold such trial. Such a trial, if approved, may be held either in conjunction with a dog show or as a separate event. If the club is not a member of The American Kennel Club, it shall pay a license fee for the privilege of holding such trial, the amount of which shall be determined by the Board of Directors of The American Kennel Club. If the club fails to hold its trial at the time and place which have been approved, the amount of the license fee paid will be returned.

Section 2. *Dog Show and Specialty Clubs.* A dog show club may be granted permission to hold a licensed or member obedience trial at its dog show, and a specialty club may also be granted permission to hold a licensed or member obedience trial if, in the opinion of the Board of Directors of The American Kennel Club, such clubs are qualified to do so.

Section 3. *Obedience Classes.* A licensed or member obedience trial need not include all of the regular obedience classes defined in this chapter, but a club will be approved to hold Open classes only if it also holds Novice classes, and a club will be approved to hold a Utility class only if it also holds Novice and Open classes. A specialty club which has been approved to hold a licensed or member obedience trial, if qualified in the opinion of the Board of Directors of The American Kennel Club, or an obedience club which has been approved to hold a licensed or member obedience trial may, subject to the approval of The American Kennel Club, offer additional non-regular classes for dogs not less than six months of age, provided a clear and complete description of the eligibility requirements and performance requirements for each such class appears in the premium list. Pre-Novice classes will not be approved at licensed or member obedience trials.

Section 4. *Tracking Tests.* A club that has been approved to hold licensed or member obedience trials and that meets the requirements of The American Kennel Club, may also make application to hold a Tracking Test. A club may not hold a tracking test on the same day as its show or obedience trial, but the tracking test may be announced in the premium list for the show or trial, and the tracking test entries may be included in the show or obedience trial catalog. If the entries are not listed in the catalog for the show or obedience trial, the club must provide, at the tracking test, several copies of a sheet, which may be typewritten, giving all the information that would be contained in the catalog for each entered dog. If the tracking test is to be held within seven days of the obedience trial the entries must be sent to the same person designated to receive the obedience trial entries, and the same closing date should apply. If the tracking test is not to be held within seven days of the obedience trial, the club may name someone else in the premium list to receive the tracking test entries, and may specify a different closing date for entries at least seven days before the tracking test.

The presence of a veterinarian shall not be required at a tracking test.

Section 5. *Obedience Trial Committee.* If an obedience trial is held by an obedience club, an Obedience Trial Committee must be appointed by the club, and this committee shall exercise all the authority vested in a dog show's Bench Show Committee. If an obedience club holds its obedience trial in conjunction with a dog show, then the Obedience Trial Committee shall have sole jurisdiction only over those dogs entered in the obedience trial, and their handlers and owners; provided, however, that if any dog is entered in both obedience and breed classes, then the Obedience Trial Committee shall have jurisdiction over such dog, its owner, and its handler, only in matters pertaining to the Obedience Regulations, and the Bench Show Committee shall have jurisdiction over such dog, its owner, and its handler, in all other matters.

When an obedience trial is to be held in conjunction with a dog show by the club which has been granted permission to hold the show, the club's Bench Show Committee shall include one person designated as "Obedience Chairman." At such event the Bench Show Committee of the show-giving club shall have sole jurisdiction over all matters which may properly come before it, regardless of whether the matter has to do with the dog show or with the obedience trial.

Section 6. *Sanctioned Matches.* A club may hold an Obedience Match by obtaining the sanction of The American Kennel Club. Sanctioned obedience matches shall be governed by such regulations as may be adopted by the Board of Directors of The American Kennel Club. Scores awarded at such matches will not be entered in the records of The American Kennel Club nor count towards an obedience title.

All of these Obedience Regulations shall also apply to sanctioned matches except for those sections in which it is specified that the provisions apply to licensed or member trials, and except where specifically stated otherwise in the Regulations for Sanctioned Matches.

Section 7. *American Kennel Club Sanction.* American Kennel Club sanction must be obtained by any club that holds American Kennel Club obedience trials, for any type of match for which it solicits or accepts entries from non-members.

Section 8. *Dog Show Rules.* All the Dog Show Rules, where applicable, shall govern the conducting of obedience trials and tracking tests, and shall apply to all persons and dogs participating in them except as these Obedience Regulations may provide otherwise.

Section 9. *Immediate Family.* As used in this chapter, "immediate family" means husband, wife, father, mother, son, daughter, brother, or sister.

Section 10. *Pure-Bred Dogs Only.* As used in these regulations the word "dog" refers to either sex but only to dogs that are pure-bred of a breed eligible for registration in The American Kennel Club stud book or for entry in the Miscellaneous class at The American Kennel Club dog shows, as only such dogs may compete in obedience trials, tracking tests, or unsanctioned matches. A judge must report to The American Kennel Club after the trial or tracking test any dog shown under him which in his opinion appears not to be pure-bred.

Section 11. *Unregistered Dogs.* Chapter 16, Section 1 of the Dog Show Rules shall apply to entries in licensed or member obedience trials and tracking tests, except that an eligible unregistered dog for which an ILP number has been issued by The American Kennel Club may be entered indefinitely in such events provided the ILP number is shown on each entry form.

Section 12. *Dogs That May Not Compete.* No dog belonging wholly or in part to a judge or to a Show or Obedience Trial

Secretary, Superintendent, or veterinarian, or to any member of such person's immediate family or household, shall be entered in any dog show, obedience trial, or tracking test at which such person officiates or is scheduled to officiate. This applies to both obedience and dog show judges when an obedience trial is held in conjunction with a dog show. However, a tracking test shall be considered a separate event for the purpose of this section.

No dog shall be entered or shown under a judge at an obedience trial or tracking test if the dog has been owned, sold, held under lease, handled in the ring, boarded, or has been regularly trained or instructed, within one year prior to the date of the obedience trial or tracking test, by the judge or by any member of his immediate family or household, and no such dog shall be eligible to compete. "Trained or instructed" applies equally to judges who train individual dogs or who train or instruct dogs in classes with or through their handlers.

Section 13. *When Titles Are Won.* Where any of the following sections of the regulations excludes from a particular obedience class dogs that have won a particular obedience title, eligibility to enter that class shall be determined as follows: a dog may continue to be shown in such a class after its handler has been notified by three different judges that it has received three qualifying scores for such title, but may not be entered or shown in such a class in any obedience trial of which the closing date for entries occurs after the owner has received official notification from The American Kennel Club that the dog has won the particular obedience title.

Where any of the following sections of the regulations requires that a dog shall have won a particular obedience title before competing in a particular obedience class, a dog may not be shown in such class at any obedience trial before the owner has received official notification from The American Kennel Club that the dog has won the required title.

Section 14. *Disqualification and Ineligibility.* A dog that is blind or deaf or that has been changed in appearance by artificial means (except for such changes as are customarily approved for its breed) may not compete in any obedience trial or tracking test and must be disqualified. Blind means having useful vision in neither eye. Deaf means without useful hearing.

If a judge has evidence of any of these conditions in any dog he is judging at an obedience trial he must, before proceeding with the judging, notify the Superintendent or Show or Trial Secretary and must call an official veterinarian to examine the dog in the ring and give to the judge an advisory opinion in writing on the condition of the dog. Only after he has seen the opinion of the veterinarian in writing shall the judge render his own decision and record it in the judge's book, marking the dog disqualified and stating the reason if he determines that disqualification is required under this section. The judge's decision is final and need not necessarily agree with the veterinarian's opinion. The written opinion of the veterinarian shall in all cases be forwarded to The American Kennel Club by the Superintendent or Show or Trial Secretary.

The judge must disqualify any dog that attempts to attack any person in the ring. He may excuse a dog that attacks another dog or that appears dangerous to other dogs in the ring. He shall mark the dog disqualified or excused and state the reason in his judge's book, and shall give the Superintendent or Show or Trial Secretary a brief report of the dog's actions which shall be submitted to The American Kennel Club with the report of the show or trial.

When a dog has been disqualified under this section as being blind or deaf or having been changed in appearance by artificial means or for having attempted to attack a person in the ring, all awards made to the dog at the trial shall be cancelled by The American Kennel Club and the dog may not again compete unless and until, following application by the owner to The American Kennel Club, the owner has received official notification from The American Kennel Club that the dog's eligibility has been reinstated.

Spayed bitches, castrated dogs, monorchid or cryptorchid males, and dogs that have faults which would disqualify them under the standards for their breeds, may compete in obedience trials if otherwise eligible under these regulations.

A dog that is lame in the ring at any obedience trial or at a tracking test may not compete and shall not receive any score at the trial. It shall be the judge's responsibility to determine whether a dog is lame. He shall not obtain the opinion of the show veterinarian. If in the judge's opinion a dog in the ring is lame, he shall not score such dog, and shall promptly excuse it from the ring and mark his book "Excused—lame."

No dog shall be eligible to compete if it appears to have been dyed or colored in any way or if the coat shows evidence of chalk or powder, or if the dog has anything attached to it whether for medical or corrective purposes, for protection, for adornment, or for any other reason, except for Maltese, Poodles, Shih Tzu, and Yorkshire Terriers which may be shown with the hair over the eyes tied back as they are normally shown in the breed ring. The judge, at his sole discretion, may agree to judge such a dog at a later time if the offending condition has been corrected.

An obedience judge is not required to be familiar with the breed standards nor to scrutinize each dog as in dog show judging, but shall be alert for conditions which may require disqualification or exclusion under this section.

Section 15. *Disturbances.* Bitches in season are not permitted to compete. The judge of an obedience trial or tracking test must remove from competition any bitch in season, any dog which its handler cannot control, any handler who interferes willfully with another competitor or his dog, and any handler who abuses his dog in the ring, and may excuse from competition any dog which he considers unfit to compete, or any bitch which appears so attractive to males as to be a disturbing element. In case of doubt an official veterinarian shall be called to give his opinion. If a dog or handler is expelled or excused by a judge, the reason shall be stated in the judge's book or in a separate report.

Section 16. *Novice A Class.* The Novice A class shall be for dogs not less than six months of age that have not won the title C.D. (Companion Dog). No person who has previously handled a dog that has won a Companion Dog title in the obedience ring at a licensed or member trial, and no person who has regularly trained such a dog, may enter or handle a dog in this class. Each dog in the class must have a separate handler, who must be its owner or a member of the owner's immediate family. The same person must handle each dog in all exercises.

Section 17. *Novice B Class.* The Novice B class shall be for dogs not less than six months of age that have not won the title C.D. Dogs in this class may be handled by the owner or any other person. A person may handle more than one dog in this class, but each dog must have a separate handler for the Long Sit and Long Down exercises when judged in the same group. No dog may be entered in both Novice A and Novice B classes at any one trial.

Section 18. *Novice Exercises and Scores.* The exercises and maximum scores in the Novice classes are:

1. Heel on Leash	35	points
2. Stand for Examination	30	points
3. Heel Free	45	points
4. Recall	30	points
5. Long Sit	30	points
6. Long Down	30	points
Maximum Total Score	200	points

Section 19. *C.D. Title.* The American Kennel Club will issue a Companion Dog certificate for each registered dog, and will permit the use of the letters "C.D." after the name of each dog that has been certified by three different judges to have received scores of more than 50% of the available points in each of the six exercises and final scores of 170 or more points in Novice classes at three licensed or member obedience trials, provided the sum total of dogs that actually competed in the regular Novice classes at each trial is not less than six.

Section 20. *Open A Class.* The Open A class shall be for dogs that have won the C.D. title but have not won the title C.D.X. (Companion Dog Excellent). Obedience judges and licensed handlers may not enter or handle dogs in this class. Each dog must be handled by its owner or by a member of his immediate family. Owners may enter more than one dog in this class but the same person who handled each dog in the first five exercises must handle the same dog in the Long Sit and Long Down exercises, except that if a person has handled more than one dog in the first five exercises he must have an additional handler, who must be the owner or a member of his immediate family, for each additional dog, when more than one dog he has handled in the first five exercises is judged in the same group for the Long Sit and Long Down.

Section 21. *Open B Class.* The Open B class will be for dogs that have won the title C.D. or C.D.X. A dog may continue to compete in this class after it has won the title U.D. (Utility Dog). Dogs in this class may be handled by the owner or by any other person. Owners may enter more than one dog in this class but the same person who handled each dog in the first five exercises must handle each dog in the Long Sit and Long Down exercises, except that if a person has handled more than one dog in the first five exercises he must have an additional handler for each additional dog, when more than one dog that he has handled in the first five exercises is judged in the same group for the Long Sit and Long Down. No dog may be entered in both Open A and Open B classes at any one trial.

Section 22. *Open Exercises and Scores.* The exercises and maximum scores in the Open classes are:

1. Heel Free	40	points
2. Drop on Recall	30	points
3. Retrieve on the Flat	25	points
4. Retrieve over High Jump	35	points
5. Broad Jump	20	points
6. Long Sit	25	points
7. Long Down	25	points
Maximum Total Score	200	points

Section 23. *C.D.X. Title.* The American Kennel Club will issue a Companion Dog Excellent certificate for each registered dog, and will permit the use of the letters "C.D.X." after the name of each dog that has been certified by three different judges of obedience trials to have received scores of more than 50% of the available

points in each of the seven exercises and final scores of 170 or more points in Open classes at three licensed or member obedience trials, provided the sum total of dogs that actually competed in the regular Open classes at each trial is not less than six.

Section 24. *Utility Class.* The Utility class shall be for dogs that have won the title C.D.X. Dogs that have won the title U.D. may continue to compete in this class. Dogs in this class may be handled by the owner or any other person. Owners may enter more than one dog in this class, but each dog must have a separate handler for the Group Examination when judged in the same group.

Section 25. *Division of Utility Class.* A club may choose to divide the Utility class into Utility A and Utility B classes, provided such division is approved by The American Kennel Club and is announced in the premium list. When this is done the Utility A class shall be for dogs which have won the title C.D.X. and have not won the title U.D. Obedience judges and licensed handlers may not enter or handle dogs in this class. A dog may be handled in the Group Examination by a person other than the person who handled it in the individual exercises, but each dog must be handled in all exercises by the owner or by a member of his immediate family. All other dogs that are eligible for the Utility class but not eligible for the Utility A class may be entered only in the Utility B class to which the conditions listed in Section 24 shall apply. No dog may be entered in both Utility A and Utility B classes at any one trial.

Section 26. *Utility Exercises and Scores.* The exercises and maximum scores in the Utility classes are:

1. Scent Discrimination—Article No. 1	30	points
2. Scent Discrimination—Article No. 2	30	points
3. Directed Retrieve	30	points
4. Signal Exercise	35	points
5. Directed Jumping	40	points
6. Group Examination	35	points
Maximum Total Score	200	points

Section 27. *U.D. Title.* The American Kennel Club will issue a Utility Dog certificate for each registered dog, and will permit the use of the letters "U.D." after the name of each dog that has been certified by three different judges of obedience trials to have received scores of more than 50% of the available points in each of the six exercises and final scores of 170 or more points in Utility classes at three licensed or member obedience trials in each of which three or more dogs actually competed in the Utility class or classes.

Section 28. *Tracking Test.* This test shall be for dogs not less than six months of age, and must be judged by two judges. With each entry form for a licensed or member tracking test for a dog that has not passed an American Kennel Club tracking test there must be filed an original written statement, dated within six months of the date the entry is received, signed by a person who has been approved by The American Kennel Club to judge tracking tests, certifying that the dog is considered by him to be ready for such a test. These original statements cannot be used again and must be submitted to The American Kennel Club with the entry forms. Written permission to waive or modify this requirement may be granted by The American Kennel Club in unusual circumstances. Tracking tests are open to all dogs that are otherwise eligible under these regulations.

This test cannot be given at a dog show or obedience trial. The duration of this test may be one day or more within a fifteen-day period after the original date in the event of an unusually large entry or other unforeseen emergency, provided that the change of date is satisfactory to the exhibitors affected.

Section 29. *T.D. Title.* The American Kennel Club will issue a Tracking Dog certificate to a registered dog, and will permit the use of the letters "T.D." after the name of each dog which has been certified by the two judges to have passed a licensed or member tracking test in which at least three dogs actually competed.

The owner of a dog holding both the U.D. and T.D. titles may use the letters "U.D.T." after the name of the dog, signifying "Utility Dog Tracker."

Section 30. *Obedience Ribbons.* At licensed or member obedience trials the following colors shall be used for prize ribbons or rosettes in all regular classes:

First Prize	Blue
Second Prize	Red
Third Prize	Yellow
Fourth Prize	White
Special Prize	Dark Green

and the following colors shall be used for non-regular classes:

First Prize	Rose
Second Prize	Brown
Third Prize	Light Green
Fourth Prize	Gray

Each ribbon or rosette shall be at least two inches wide and approximately eight inches long, and shall bear on its face a facsimile of the seal of The American Kennel Club, the words "Obedience Trial," the name of the prize, the name of the trial-giving club, the date of the trial, and the name of the city or town where the trial is given.

Section 31. *Match Ribbons.* If ribbons are given at sanctioned obedience matches they shall be of the following colors and shall have the words "Obedience Match" printed on them, but may be of any design or size:

First Prize	Rose
Second Prize	Brown
Third Prize	Light Green
Fourth Prize	Gray
Special Prize	Green with pink edges

Section 32. *Prizes.* Ribbons for the four official placings, and all other prizes offered for competition within a single regular class

at a licensed or member trial, shall be awarded only to dogs that earn scores of more than 50% of the available points in each exercise and final scores of 170 or more points.

Prizes for which dogs in one class compete against dogs in one or more other classes at a licensed or member trial may, at the option of the club holding the trial, specify that scores of more than 50% of the available points in each exercise and final scores of 170 or more points are required.

Ribbons and all prizes offered at sanctioned obedience matches, and in non-regular classes at licensed and member trials, shall be awarded on the basis of final scores without regard to more than 50% of the points in each exercise.

Prizes at a licensed or member obedience trial must be offered to be won outright, with the exception that a prize which requires three wins by the same owner, not necessarily with the same dog, for permanent possession, may be offered for the dog with the highest qualifying score in one of the regular classes, for the highest scoring dog in the regular classes, or for the highest combined score in the Open B and Utility classes.

Subject to the provisions of paragraphs one and two of this section, prizes may be offered for the highest scoring dogs of the Groups as defined in Chapter 2 of the Dog Show Rules, or for the highest scoring dogs of any breeds, but not for a breed variety. Show varieties are not recognized for obedience. In accordance with Chapter 2, all Poodles are in the Non-Sporting Group and all Manchester Terriers are in the Terrier Group.

Prizes offered only to members of certain clubs or organizations will not be approved for publication in premium lists.

Section 33. *Risk.* The owner or agent entering a dog in an obedience trial does so at his own risk and agrees to abide by the rules of The American Kennel Club, and the Obedience Regulations.

Section 34. *Decisions.* At the trial the decisions of the judge shall be final in all matters affecting the scoring and the working of the dogs and their handlers. The Obedience Trial Committee, or the Bench Show Committee if the trial is held by a show-giving club, shall decide all other matters arising at the trial, including protests against dogs made under Chapter 20 of the Dog Show Rules, subject, however, to the rules and regulations of The American Kennel Club.

Section 35. *Dogs Must Compete.* Any dog entered and received at a licensed or member obedience trial must compete in all exercises of all classes in which it is entered unless disqualified, expelled, or excused by the judge or by the Bench Show or Obedience Trial Committee, or unless excused by the official veterinarian to protect the health of the dog or of other dogs at the trial. The excuse of the official veterinarian must be in writing and must be approved by the Superintendent or Show or Trial Secretary and must be submitted to The American Kennel Club with the report of the trial. The judge must report to The American Kennel Club any dog that is not brought back for the group exercises.

Section 36. *Judging Program.* Any club holding a licensed or member obedience trial must prepare, after the entries have closed, a program showing the time scheduled for the judging of each of the classes. A copy of this program shall be mailed to the owner of each entered dog and to each judge, and the program shall be printed in the catalog. This program shall be based on the judging of no more than eight Novice entries, seven Open entries, or five Utility entries, per hour during the time the show or trial will be open as published in the premium list, taking into consideration the starting hour for judging if published in the premium list, and the availability of rings. No judge shall be scheduled to exceed this rate of judging. In addition, one hour for rest or meals must be allowed if, under this formula, it will take more than five hours of actual judging to judge the dogs entered under him. No judge shall be assigned to judge for more than eight hours in one day under this formula, including any breed-judging assignment if the obedience trial is held in conjunction with a dog show.

If any non-regular class is to be judged in the same ring as any regular class, or by the judge of any regular class, the non-regular class must be judged after the regular class.

Section 37. *Limitation of Entries.* If a club anticipates an entry in excess of its facilities for a licensed or member trial, it may limit entries in any or all regular classes, but non-regular classes will not be approved if the facilities are limited; or a club may limit entries in any or all regular classes to 64 in a Novice class, 56 in an Open class, or 40 in a Utility class.

Prominent announcement of such limits must appear on the title or cover page of the premium list for an obedience trial or immediately under the obedience heading in the premium list for a dog show, with a statement that entries in one or more specified classes or in the obedience trial will automatically close when a certain limit or limits have been reached, even though the official closing date for entries has not arrived.

Section 38. *Additional Judges, Reassignment, Split Classes.* If when the entries have closed, it is found that the entry under one or more judges exceeds the limit established in Section 36, the club shall immediately secure the approval of The American Kennel Club for the appointment of one or more additional judges, or for reassignment of its advertised judges, so that no judge will be required to exceed the limit.

If a judge with an excessive entry was advertised to judge more than one class, one or more of his classes shall be assigned to another judge. The class or classes selected for reassignment shall first be any non-regular classes for which he was advertised, and shall then be either the regular class or classes with the minimum number of entries, or those with the minimum scheduled time, which will bring the advertised judge's schedule within, and as close as possible to, the maximum limit. If a judge with an excessive entry was advertised to judge only one class, the Superintendent, Show Secretary, or Obedience Trial Secretary shall divide the entry as evenly as possible between the advertised judge and the other judge by drawing lots.

The club shall promptly mail to the owner of each entry affected, a notification of any change of judge. The owner shall be permitted to withdraw such entry at any time prior to the day of the show, and the entry fee shall then be refunded. If the entry in any one class is split in this manner, the advertised judge shall judge the run-off of any tie scores that may develop between the two groups of dogs, after each judge has first run-off any ties resulting from his own judging.

Section 39. *Split Classes in Premium List.* A club may choose to announce two or more judges for any class in its premium list. In such case the entries shall be divided by lots as provided above. The identification slips and judging program shall be made up so that the owner of each dog will know the division, and the judge of the division, in which his dog is entered, but no owner shall be entitled to a refund of entry fee. In such case the premium list shall also specify the judge for the run-off of any tie scores which may develop between the dogs in the different groups, after each judge has first run-off any ties resulting from his own judging.

Section 40. *Split Classes, Official Ribbons.* A club which gives a split class, whether the split is announced in the premium list or made after entries have closed, shall not award American Kennel Club official ribbons in either section, but may offer prizes on the basis of qualifying scores made within each section if the split class is announced in the premium list. The four dogs with the highest qualifying scores in the class, regardless of the section in which they were made, shall be called back into the ring and awarded the four American Kennel Club official ribbons by one of the judges of the class who shall be responsible for recording the entry numbers of the four placed dogs in one of the judges' books.

Section 41. *Training of Dogs.* There shall be no drilling nor intensive or corrective training of dogs on the grounds or premises at a licensed or member obedience trial. No practice rings or areas shall be permitted at such events. All dogs shall be kept on leash except when in the obedience ring or exercise ring. Spiked or other special training collars shall not be used on the grounds or premises at an obedience trial or match. These requirements shall not be interpreted as preventing a handler from moving normally about the grounds or premises with his dog at heel on leash, nor from giving such signals or such commands in a normal tone, as are necessary and usual in everyday life in heeling a dog or making it stay, but physical or verbal disciplining of dogs shall not be permitted except to a reasonable extent in the case of an attack on a person or another dog. The Superintendent, or Show or Trial Secretary, and the members of the Bench Show or Obedience Trial Committee, shall be responsible for compliance with this section, and shall investigate any reports of infractions.

Section 42. *Abuse of Dogs.* The Bench Show or Obedience Trial Committee shall also investigate any reports of abuse of dogs or severe disciplining of dogs on the grounds or premises of a show, trial, or match. Any person who, at a licensed or member obedience trial, conducts himself in such manner or in any other manner prejudicial to the best interests of the sport, or who fails to comply with the requirements of Section 41 above after receiving a warning, shall be dealt with promptly, during the trial if possible, after the offender has been notified of the specific charges against him, and has been given an opportunity to be heard in his own defense in accordance with Section 43 below.

Article XII Section 2 of the Constitution and By-Laws of The American Kennel Club provides:

Section 43. *Discipline.* The Bench Show, Obedience Trial, or Field Trial Committee of a club or association shall have the right to suspend any person from the privileges of The American Kennel Club for conduct prejudicial to the best interests of pure-bred dogs, dog shows, obedience trials, field trials, or The American Kennel Club, alleged to have occurred in connection with or during the progress of its show, obedience trial, or field trial, after the alleged offender has been given an opportunity to be heard.

Notice in writing must be sent promptly by registered mail by the Bench Show, Obedience Trial, or Field Trial Committee to the person suspended and a duplicate notice giving the name and address of the person suspended and full details as to the reasons for the suspension must be forwarded to The American Kennel Club within seven days.

An appeal may be taken from a decision of a Bench Show, Obedience Trial, or Field Trial Committee. Notice in writing claiming such appeal together with a deposit of five ($5.00) dollars must be sent to The American Kennel Club within thirty days after the date of suspension. The Board of Directors may itself hear said appeal or may refer to a committee of the Board, or to a Trial Board to be heard. The deposit shall become the property of The American Kennel Club if the decision is confirmed, or shall be returned to the appellant if the decision is not confirmed.

(See "Guide for Bench Show and Obedience Trial Committees in Dealing with Misconduct at Dog Shows and Obedience Trials" for proper procedure at licensed or member obedience trials.)

(The Committee at a Sanctioned event does not have this power of suspension, but must investigate any allegation of such conduct and forward a complete and detailed report of any such incident to The American Kennel Club.)

CHAPTER 2

Regulations for Performance

Section 1. *Ring Conditions.* If the judging takes place indoors, the ring should be rectangular and should be about 35' wide and 50' long for all obedience classes. In no case shall the ring for a Utility class be less than 35' by 50', and in no case shall the ring for a Novice or Open class be less than 30' by 40'. The floor shall have a surface or covering that provides firm footing for the largest dogs, and rubber or similar non-slip material must be laid for the take off and landing at all jumps unless the surface, in the judge's opinion, is such as not to require it. At an outdoor show or trial the rings shall be about 40' wide and 50' long. The ground shall be clean and level, and the grass, if any, shall be cut short. The Club and Superintendent are responsible for providing, for the Open classes, an appropriate place approved by the judge, for the handlers to go completely out of sight of their dogs. If inclement weather at an outdoor trial necessitates the judging of obedience under shelter, the requirements as to ring size may be waived.

Section 2. *Obedience Rings at Dog Shows.* At an outdoor dog show a separate ring or rings shall be provided for obedience, and a sign forbidding anyone to permit any dog to use the ring, except when being judged, shall be set up in each such ring by the Superintendent or Show Secretary. It shall be his duty as well as that of the Show Committee to enforce this regulation. At an indoor show where limited space does not permit the exclusive use of any ring for obedience, the same regulation will apply after the obedience rings have been set up. At a dog show the material used for enclosing the obedience rings for the regular classes shall be at least equal to the material used for enclosing the breed rings. The ring must be thoroughly cleaned before the obedience judging starts if it has previously been used for breed judging.

Section 3. *Compliance with Regulations and Standards.* In accordance with the certification on the entry form, the handler of each dog and the person signing each entry form must be familiar with the Obedience Regulations applicable to the class in which the dog is entered. A handler with a physical handicap may compete, provided he can move himself about the ring as required, without physical assistance or guidance from another person, except for guidance to the proper location in the ring which may be given by the judge, or, in the group exercises, by a person who is handling a competing dog in the ring.

Section 4. *Praise and Handling between Exercises.* Praise and patting are allowed between exercises, but points must be deducted from the total score for a dog that is not under reasonable control while being praised. A handler must not carry or offer food in the ring.

Imperfections in heeling between exercises will not be judged. In the Novice classes the dog may be guided gently by the collar between exercises and to get it into proper position for the next exercise. There shall be a substantial penalty for any dog that is picked up or carried at any time in the obedience ring, and for a dog in the Open or Utility classes that is not readily controllable or that is physically controlled at any time, except for permitted patting between exercises, and posing, or if the judge requests the handler to hold his dog for measuring. Minor penalties shall be imposed for a dog that does not respond promptly to its handler's commands or signals between exercises in the Open and Utility classes.

Section 5. *Use of Leash.* All dogs shall be kept on leash except when in the obedience ring or exercise ring. Dogs should be brought into the ring and taken out of the ring on leash. Dogs may be kept on leash in the ring when brought in to receive awards, and when waiting in the ring before and after the group exercises. The leash shall be left on the judge's table between the individual exercises, and during all exercises except the Heel on Leash and group exercises. The leash may be of fabric or leather and, in the Novice classes, shall be of sufficient length to provide adequate slack in the Heel on Leash exercise.

Section 6. *Collars.* Dogs in the obedience ring must wear well-fitting plain buckle or slip collars of leather, fabric, or chain. Fancy collars, spiked collars or other special training collars, or collars that are either too tight or so large that they hang down unreasonably in front of the dogs, are not permitted, nor may there be anything hanging from the collars.

Section 7. *Misbehavior.* Any disciplining by the handler in the ring, any display of fear or nervousness by the dog, or any uncontrolled behavior of the dog such as snapping, barking, relieving itself in the ring, or running away from its handler, whether it occurs during an exercise, between exercises, or before or after judging, must be penalized according to the seriousness of the misbehavior, and the judge may expel or excuse the dog from further competition in the class. If such behavior occurs during an exercise, the penalty must first be applied to the score for that exercise. Should the penalty be greater than the value of the exercise during which it is incurred, the additional points shall be deducted from the total score under Misbehavior. If such behavior occurs before or after the judging or between exercises, the entire penalty shall be deducted from the total score.

Section 8. *Commands and Signals.* Whenever a command or signal is mentioned in these regulations, a single command or signal only may be given by the handler, and any extra commands or signals must be penalized; except that whenever the regulations specify "command and/or signal" the handler may give either one or the other or both command and signal simultaneously. When a signal is permitted and given, it must be a single gesture with one arm and hand only, and the arm must immediately be returned to a natural position. Delay in following a judge's order to give a command or signal must be penalized, unless the delay is directed by the judge because of some distraction or interference.

The signal for downing a dog may be given either with the arm raised or with a down swing of the arm, but any pause in holding the arm upright followed by a down swing of the arm will be considered an additional signal.

Signaling correction to a dog is forbidden and must be penalized. Signals must be inaudible and the handler must not touch the dog. Any unusual noise or motion may be considered to be a signal. Movements of the body shall be considered additional signals except that a handler may bend as far as necessary to bring his hand on a level with the dog's eyes in giving a signal to a dog in the heel position, and that in the Directed Retrieve exercise the body and knees may be bent to the extent necessary to give the direction to the dog. Whistling or the use of a whistle is prohibited.

The dog's name may be used once immediately before any verbal command or before a verbal command and signal when these regulations permit command and/or signal. The name shall not be used with any signal not given simultaneously with a verbal command. The dog's name, when given immediately before a verbal command, shall not be considered as an additional command, but a dog that responds to its name without waiting for the verbal command shall be scored as having anticipated the command. The dog should never anticipate the handler's directions, but must wait for the appropriate commands and/or signals. Moving forward at heel without any command or signal other than the natural movement of the handler's left leg, shall not be considered as anticipation.

Loud commands by handlers to their dogs create a poor impression of obedience and should be avoided. Shouting is not necessary even in a noisy place if the dog is properly trained to respond to a normal tone of voice. Commands which in the judge's opinion are excessively loud will be penalized.

Section 9.   *Heel Position*. The heel position as used in these regulations, whether the dog is sitting, standing, or moving at heel, means that the dog shall be straight in line with the direction in which the handler is facing, at the handler's left side, and as close as practicable to the handler's left leg without crowding, permitting the handler freedom of motion at all times. The area from the dog's head to shoulder shall be in line with the handler's left hip.

Section 10.   *Heel on Leash*. The handler shall enter the ring with his dog on a loose leash and shall stand still with the dog sitting in the heel position until the judge asks if the handler is ready and then gives the order "Forward." The handler may give the command or signal to Heel, and shall start walking briskly and in a natural manner with the dog on loose leash. The dog shall walk close to the left side of the handler without crowding, permitting the handler freedom of motion at all times. At each order to "Halt," the handler will stop and his dog shall sit straight and smartly in the Heel position without command or signal and shall not move until the handler again moves forward on order from the judge. It is permissible after each Halt before moving again, for the handler to give the command or signal to Heel.

The leash may be held in either hand or in both hands, at the handler's option, provided the hands are in a natural position. However, the handler and the dog will be penalized if, in the judge's opinion, the leash is used to signal or give assistance to the dog.

Any tightening or jerking of the leash or any act, signal, or command which in the opinion of the judge gives the dog assistance shall be penalized. The judge will give the order "Forward," "Halt," "Right turn," "Fast," "Left turn," "About turn," "Slow," "Normal," which order signifies that both the handler and dog must run, changing pace and moving forward at noticeably accelerated speed. These orders may be given in any sequence and may be repeated if necessary. In executing the About Turn, the handler will do a Right About Turn in all cases. The judge will say "Exercise finished" after the heeling, and then "Are you ready?" before starting the Figure Eight.

The judge will order the handler to execute the "Figure Eight" which signifies that the handler may give the command or signal to Heel and, with his dog in the heel position, shall walk around and between the two stewards who shall stand about eight feet apart or, if there is only one steward, shall walk around and between the judge and the steward. The Figure Eight in the Novice classes shall be done on leash only. The handler may choose to go in either direction. There shall be no About Turn in the Figure Eight, but the handler and dog shall go twice completely around the Figure Eight with at least one Halt during and another Halt at the end of the exercise.

Section 11. *Stand for Examination.* The judge will give the order for examination and the handler, without further order from the judge, will stand or pose his dog off leash, give the command and/or signal to Stay, walk forward about six feet in front of his dog, turn around, and stand facing his dog. The method by which the dog is made to stand or pose is optional with the handler who may take any reasonable time in posing the dog, as in the show ring, before deciding to give the command and/or signal to Stay. The judge will approach the dog from the front and will touch its head, body, and hindquarters only, and will then give the order "Back to your dog," whereupon the handler will walk around behind his dog to the heel position. The dog must remain in a standing position until the judge says "Exercise finished." The dog must show no shyness nor resentment at any time during the exercise.

Section 12. *Heel Free.* This shall be executed in the same manner as Heel on Leash except that the dog is off the leash. Heeling in both Novice and Open classes is done in the same manner except that in the Open classes all work is done off leash, including the Figure Eight.

Section 13. *Recall and Drop on Recall.* To execute the Recall to handler, upon order or signal from the judge to "Leave your dog," the dog is given the command and/or signal to stay in the sitting position while the handler walks forward about 35 feet towards the other end of the ring, turns around, and faces his dog. Upon order or signal from the judge to "Call your dog," the handler calls or signals the dog, which in the Novice class must come straight in at a brisk pace and sit straight, centered immediately in front of the handler's feet and close enough so that the handler could readily touch its head without moving either foot or having to stretch forward. The dog shall not touch the handler nor sit between his feet. Upon order or signal from the judge to "Finish," the dog on command or signal must go smartly to the heel position and sit. The method by which the dog goes to the heel position shall be optional with the handler provided it is done smartly and the dog sits straight at heel.

In the Open class, at a point designated by the judge, the dog must drop completely to a down position immediately on command or signal from the handler, and must remain in the down position until, on order or signal from the judge, the handler calls or signals the dog, which must rise and complete the exercise as in the Novice class.

Section 14. *Long Sit.* In the Long Sit in the Novice classes all the competing dogs in the class take the exercise together, except that if there are twelve or more dogs they shall, at the judge's option, be judged in groups of not less than six nor more than fifteen dogs. Where the same judge does both classes the separate classes may be combined provided there are not more than fifteen dogs competing in the two classes combined. The dogs that are in the ring shall be lined up in catalog order along one of the four sides of the ring. Handlers' armbands, weighted with leashes or other articles if necessary, shall be placed behind the dogs. On order from the judge the handlers shall sit their dogs, if they are not already sitting, and on further order from the judge to "Leave your dogs" the handlers shall give the command and/or signal to Stay and immediately leave their dogs, go to the opposite side of the ring, and line up facing their respective dogs. After one minute from the time he has ordered the handlers to leave their dogs, the judge will order the handlers "Back to your dogs" whereupon the handlers must return promptly to their dogs, each walking around in back of his own dog to the heel position. The dogs must not move from the sitting position until after the judge says "Exercise finished."

Section 15. *Long Down.* The Long Down in the Novice classes is done in the same manner as the Long Sit except that instead of sitting the dogs the handlers, on order from the judge, will down their dogs without touching the dogs or their collars, and except further that the judge will order the handlers back after three minutes. The dogs must stay in the down position until after the judge says "Exercise finished."

Section 16. *Open Classes, Long Sit, and Long Down.* These exercises in the Open classes are performed in the same manner as in the Novice classes except that after leaving their dogs the handlers must cross to the opposite side of the ring, and then leave the ring in single file as directed by the judge and go to a place designated by the judge, completely out of sight of their dogs, where they must remain until called by the judge after the expiration of the time limit of three minutes in the Long Sit and five minutes in the Long Down, from the time the judge gave the order to "Leave your dogs." On order from the judge the handlers shall return to the ring in single file in reverse order, lining up facing their dogs at the opposite side of the ring, and returning to their dogs on order from the judge.

Section 17. *Retrieve on the Flat.* In retrieving the dumbbell on the flat, the handler stands with his dog sitting in the heel position in a place designated by the judge, and the judge gives the orders "Throw it," whereupon the handler may give the command and/or signal to Stay, which may not be given with the hand that is holding the dumbbell, and throws the dumbbell; "Send your dog," whereupon the handler gives the command or signal to his dog to retrieve; "Take it," whereupon the handler gives the command or signal to heel as in the Recall. The dog shall not move forward to retrieve nor deliver to hand on return until given the command or signal by the handler following order by the judge. The retrieve shall be executed at a fast trot or gallop, without unnecessary mouthing or playing with the dumbbell. The dog shall sit straight, centered immediately in front of its handler's feet and close enough so that the handler can readily take the dumbbell without moving either foot or having to stretch forward. The dog shall not touch the handler nor sit between his feet.

The dumbbell, which must be approved by the judge, shall be made of one or more solid pieces of one of the heavy hardwoods, which shall not be hollowed out. It may be unfinished, or coated with a clear finish, or painted white. It shall have no decorations or attachments but may bear an inconspicuous mark for identification. The size of the dumbbell shall be proportionate to the size of the dog. The judge shall require the dumbbell to be thrown again before the dog is sent if, in his opinion, it is thrown too short a distance, or too far to one side, or against the ringside.

Section 18. *Retrieve over High Jump.* In retrieving the dumbbell over the High Jump, the exercise is executed in the same manner as the Retrieve on the Flat, except that the dog must jump the High Jump both going and coming. The High Jump shall be jumped clear and the jump shall be as nearly as possible one and one-half times the height of the dog at the withers, as determined by the judge, with a minimum height of 8 inches and a maximum of 36 inches. This applies to all breeds with the following exceptions:

> The jump shall be once the height of the dog at the withers or 36 inches, whichever is less, for the following breeds—Bloodhounds, Bullmastiffs, Great Danes, Great Pyrenees, Mastiffs, Newfoundlands, St. Bernards.
>
> The jump shall be once the height of the dog at the withers or 8 inches, whichever is greater, for the following breeds—Spaniels (Clumber), Spaniels (Sussex), Dachshunds, Welsh Corgis (Cardigan), Welsh Corgis (Pem-

broke), Australian Terriers, Cairn Terriers, Dandie Dinmont Terriers, Norwich Terriers, Scottish Terriers, Sealyham Terriers, Skye Terriers, West Highland White Terriers, Maltese, Pekingese, Bulldogs, French Bulldogs.

The handler has the option of standing any reasonable distance from the High Jump, but must stay in the same spot throughout the exercise.

The side posts of the High Jump shall be four feet high and the jump shall be five feet wide and shall be so constructed as to provide adjustment for each two inches from eight inches to thirty-six inches. It is suggested that the jump have a bottom board eight inches wide including the space from the bottom of the board to the ground or floor, together with three other eight-inch boards, one four-inch board, and one two-inch board. A six-inch board may also be provided. The jump shall be painted a flat white. The width in inches, and nothing else, shall be painted on each side of each board in black two-inch figures, the figure on the bottom board representing the distance from the ground or floor to the top of the board.

Section 19. *Broad Jump*. In the Broad Jump the handler will stand with his dog sitting in the heel position in front of and anywhere within ten feet of the jump. On order from the judge to "Leave your dog," the handler will give his dog the command and/or signal to stay, and go to a position facing the right side of the jump, with his toes about two feet from the jump, and anywhere between the first and last hurdles. On order from the judge the handler shall give the command or signal to jump and the dog shall clear the entire distance of the Broad Jump without touching and, without further command or signal, return to a sitting position immediately in front of the handler as in the Recall. The handler shall change his position by executing a right-angle turn while the dog is in mid-air, but shall remain in the same spot. On order from the judge, the handler will give the command or signal to Heel and the dog shall finish as in the Recall.

The Broad Jump shall consist of four hurdles, built to telescope for convenience, made of boards about eight inches wide, the largest measuring about five feet in length and six inches high at the highest point, all painted a flat white. When set up they shall be arranged in order of size and shall be evenly spaced so as to cover a distance equal to twice the height of the High Jump as set for the particular dog, with the low side of each hurdle and the lowest hurdle nearest the dog. The four hurdles shall be used for a jump of 52″ to 72″, three for a jump of 32″ to 48″, and two for a jump of 16″ to 28″. The highest hurdles shall be removed first.

Section 20. *Scent Discrimination.* In each of these two exercises the dog must select by scent alone and retrieve an article which has been handled by its handler. The articles shall be provided by the handler and these shall consist of two sets, each comprised of five identical articles not more than six inches in length, which may be items of everyday use. One set shall be made entirely of rigid metal, and one of leather of such design that nothing but leather is visible except for the minimum amount of thread or metal necessary to hold the article together. The articles in each set must be legibly numbered each with a different number, and must be approved by the judge.

The handler shall present all ten articles to the judge and the judge shall designate one article from each of the two sets, and shall make a written note of the numbers of the two articles he selects. These two handler's articles shall be placed on a table or chair in the ring until picked up by the handler who shall hold in his hand only one article at a time. The handler's scent may be imparted to the article only from his hands which must remain in plain sight. The handler has the option as to which article he picks up first. Before the start of the Scent Discrimination exercises the judge or the steward will handle each of the remaining eight articles as he places them at random in the ring about six inches apart. The handler will stand about fifteen feet from the articles with the dog sitting in the heel position. The handler and dog will face away from the articles that are on the ground or floor from the time the judge takes the handler's article until he orders "Send your dog." On order from the judge, the handler immediately will place his article on the judge's book or work sheet and the judge, without touching the article with his hands, will place it among the other articles.

On order from the judge to "Send your dog," the handler and dog will execute a Right About Turn to face the articles and the handler will simultaneously give the command or signal to retrieve. The dog shall not again sit after turning, but shall go directly to the articles. The handler may give his scent to the dog by gently touching the dog's nose with the palm of one open hand, but this may only be done while the dog is sitting at heel, and the arm and hand must be returned to a natural position before handler and dog turn to face the articles. The dog shall go at a brisk pace to the articles. It may take any reasonable time to select the right article, but only provided it works continuously and does not pick up any article other than the one with its handler's scent. After picking up the right article the dog shall return at a brisk pace and complete the exercise as in the Retrieve on the Flat.

The same procedure is followed in each of the two Scent Discrimination exercises. Should a dog retrieve a wrong article in the first exercise, it shall be placed on the table or chair, and the handler's article must also be taken up from the remaining articles. The second exercise shall then be completed with one less article in the ring.

Section 21. *Directed Retrieve.* In this exercise the handler will provide three regular full-size, predominantly white, work gloves, which must be open and must be approved by the judge. The handler will stand with his dog sitting in the heel position, midway between and in line with the two jumps. The judge or steward will drop the three gloves across the end of the ring in view of the handler and dog, one glove in each corner and one in the center, about three feet from the end of the ring and, for the corner gloves, about three feet from the side of the ring, where all three gloves will be clearly visible to the dog and handler. There shall be no table or chair at this end of the ring.

The judge will give the order "Left" or "Right" or "Center." If the judge orders "Left" or "Right," the handler must give the command to Heel and shall pivot in place with his dog in the direction ordered, to face the designated glove. The handler shall not touch the dog to get it in position. The handler will then give his dog the direction to the designated glove with a single motion of his left hand and arm along the right side of the dog, and will give the command to retrieve either simultaneously with or immediately following the giving of the direction. The dog shall then go directly to the glove at a brisk pace and retrieve it without unnecessary mouthing or playing with it, completing the exercise as in Retrieve on the Flat.

The handler may bend his knees and body in giving the direction to the dog, after which the handler will stand erect with his arms in a natural position. The exercise shall consist of a single retrieve, but the judge shall designate different glove positions for successive dogs.

Section 22. *Signal Exercise.* In the Signal Exercise the heeling is done in the same manner as in the Heel Free exercise except that throughout the entire exercise the handler uses signals only and must not speak to his dog at any time. On order from the judge to "Forward," the handler may signal his dog to walk at heel and then, on specific order from the judge in each case, the handler and the dog execute a "Left turn," "Right turn," "About turn," "Halt," "Slow," "Normal," "Fast." These orders may be given in any sequence and may be repeated if necessary. Then on order from the judge, and while the dog is walking at heel, the handler signals his dog to Stand in the heel position near the end of the ring, and on further order from the judge to "Leave your dog," the handler signals his dog to Stay, goes to the far end of the ring, and turns to face his dog. Then on separate and specific signals from the judge in each case, the handler will give the signals to Drop, to Sit, to Come, and to Finish as in the Recall. During the heeling part of this exercise the handler may not give any signal except where a command or signal is permitted in the Heeling exercises.

Section 23. *Directed Jumping.* In the Directed Jumping exercise the jumps shall be placed midway in the ring at right angles to the side of the ring and eighteen to twenty feet apart; the Bar Jump on one side, the High Jump on the other. The handler, from a position on the center line of the ring and about twenty feet from the line of the jumps, stands with his dog sitting in the heel position. On order from the judge to "Send your dog," he commands and/or signals his dog to go forward at a brisk pace toward the other end of the ring to an equal distance beyond the jumps and in the approximate center where the handler gives the command to Sit, whereupon the dog must stop and sit with its attention on the handler, but need not sit squarely. The judge will then designate which jump is to be taken first by the dog, whereupon the handler commands and/or signals his dog to return to him over the designated jump, the dog sitting in front of the handler and finishing as in the Recall. While the dog is in mid-air the handler may turn so as to be facing the dog as it returns. The judge will say "Exercise finished" after the dog has returned to the heel position. When the dog is again sitting in the heel position for the second part of the exercise, the judge will ask "Are you ready?" before giving the order to "Send your dog" for the second jump. The same procedure is to be followed for the dog taking the opposite jump. It is optional with the judge which jump is taken first but both jumps must be taken to complete the exercise and the judge must not designate the jump until the dog is at the far end of the ring.

The height of the jumps shall be the same as required in the Open classes. The High Jump shall be the same as that used in the Open classes, and the Bar Jump shall consist of a bar between two and two and a half inches square with the four edges rounded sufficiently to remove any sharpness. The bar shall be painted a flat black and white in alternate sections of about three inches each. The bar shall be supported by two unconnected four-foot upright posts about five feet apart. The bar shall be adjustable for each two inches of height from eight inches to thirty-six inches, and the jump shall be so constructed and positioned that the bar can be knocked off without disturbing the uprights. The dog shall clear the jumps without touching them.

Section 24. *Group Examination.* All the competing dogs take this exercise together, except that if there are twelve or more dogs, they shall be judged in groups of not less than six nor more than fifteen dogs, at the judge's option. The handlers and dogs that are in the ring shall line up in catalog order, side by side down the center of the ring with the dogs in the heel position. Each handler shall place his armband, weighted with leash or other article, if necessary, behind his dog. On order from the judge to "Stand your dogs," all the handlers will stand or pose their dogs, and on order from the judge to "Leave your dogs," all the handlers will give the command and/or signal to Stay, walk forward to the side of the ring, then about turn and face their dogs. The judge will approach each dog in turn from the front and examine it, going over the dog with his hands as in dog show judging. When all dogs have been examined, and after the handlers have been away from their dogs for at least three minutes, the judge will promptly order the handlers "Back to your dogs," and the handlers will walk around behind their dogs to the heel position, after which the judge will say "Exercise finished." Each dog must remain standing at its position in the line from the time its handler leaves it until the end of the exercise, and must show no shyness nor resentment.

Section 25. *Tracking.* The tracking test must be performed with the dog on leash, the length of the track to be not less than 440 yards nor more than 500 yards, the scent to be not less than one half hour nor more than two hours old and that of a stranger who will leave an inconspicuous glove or wallet, dark in color, at the end of the track where it must be found by the dog and picked up by the dog or handler. The article must be approved in advance by the judges. The tracklayer will follow the track which has been staked out with flags a day or more earlier, collecting all the flags on the way with the exception of one flag at the start of the track to indicate the direction of the track; then deposit the article at the end of the track and leave the course, proceeding straight ahead at least fifty feet. The tracklayer must wear his own shoes which, if not having leather soles, must have uppers of fabric or leather. The dog shall wear a harness to which is attached a leash between twenty and forty feet in length. The handler shall follow the dog at a distance of not less than twenty feet, and the dog shall not be guided by the handler. The dog may be restrained by the handler, but any leading or guiding of the dog constitutes grounds for calling the handler off and marking the dog "Failed."

A dog may, at the handler's option, be given one, and only one, second chance to take the scent between the two flags, provided it has not passed the second flag.

The Club or Tracking Test Secretary, after a licensed or member tracking test, shall forward the two copies of the judges' marked charts, the entry forms with certifications attached, and a marked and certified copy of the catalog pages or sheets listing the dogs entered in the tracking test, to The American Kennel Club so as to reach its office within seven days after the close of the test.

CHAPTER 3

Regulations for Judging

Section 1. *Standardized Judging.* Standardized judging is of paramount importance. Judges are not permitted to inject their own variations into the exercises, but must see that each handler and dog executes the various exercises exactly as described in these regulations. A handler who is familiar with these regulations should be able to enter the ring under any judge without having to inquire how the particular judge wishes to have any exercise performed, and without being confronted with some unexpected requirement.

Section 2. *Handicapped Handlers.* Judges may modify the specific requirements of these regulations for handlers to the extent necessary to permit physically handicapped handlers to compete, provided such handlers can move about the ring without physical assistance or guidance from another person, except for guidance from the judge or from the handler of a competing dog in the ring for the group exercises. Dogs handled by such handlers shall be required to perform all parts of all exercises as described in these regulations, and shall be penalized for failure to perform any part of an exercise.

Section 3. *Judge's Report on Ring and Equipment.* The Superintendent and the officials of the club holding the obedience trial are responsible for providing rings and equipment which meet the requirements of these regulations. However, the judge must check the ring and equipment provided for his use before starting to judge, and must report to The American Kennel Club after the trial any undesirable ring conditions or deficiencies that have not been promptly corrected at his request.

Section 4. *Stewards.* The judge is in sole charge of his ring until his assignment is completed. Stewards are provided to assist him, but they may act only on the judge's instructions. Stewards shall not give information or instructions to owners and handlers except as specifically instructed by the judge, and then only in such a manner that it is clear that the instructions are those of the judge.

Section 5. *Training and Disciplining in the Ring.* The judge shall not permit any handler to train his dog nor to practice any exercise in the ring either before or after he is judged, and shall deduct points from the total score of any dog whose handler does this. A handler who disciplines his dog in the ring must be severely penalized. The penalty shall be deducted from the points available for the exercise during which the disciplining may occur, and additional points may be deducted from the total score if necessary. If the disciplining does not occur during an exercise the penalty shall be deducted from the total score. Any abuse of a dog in the ring must be immediately reported by the judge to the Bench Show or Obedience Trial Committee for action under Chapter 1, Section 43.

Section 6. *Catalog Order.* Dogs should be judged in catalog order to the extent that it is practicable to do so without holding up the judging in any ring for a dog that is entered in more than one class at the show or trial.

Judges are not required to wait for dogs for either the individual exercises or the group exercises. It is the responsibility of each contestant to be ready with his dog at ringside when required, without waiting to be called. The judge's first consideration should be the convenience of those exhibitors who are at ringside with their dogs when scheduled, and who ask no favors.

A judge may agree on request in advance to judge a dog earlier or later than the time scheduled by catalog order if the same dog is entered in another class which may conflict. However, a judge should not hesitate to mark absent and to refuse to judge any dog and handler that are not at ringside ready to be judged in catalog order if no such arrangement has been made in advance, nor if the dog is available while its handler is occupied with some other dog or dogs at the show or trial.

Section 7. *Judge's Book and Score Sheets.* The judge must enter the scores and sub-total score of each dog in the official judge's book immediately after each dog has been judged on the individual exercises and before judging the next dog. Scores for the group exercises and total scores must be entered in the official judge's book immediately after each group of dogs has been judged. No score may be changed except to correct an arithmetical error or if a score has been entered in the wrong column. All final scores must be entered in the judge's book before prizes are awarded. No person other than the judge may make any entry in the judge's book. Judges may use separate score sheets for their own purposes, but shall not give out nor allow exhibitors to see such sheets, nor give out any other written scores, nor permit anyone else to distribute score sheets or cards prepared by the judge. Carbon copies of the sheets in the official judge's book shall be made available through the Superintendent or Show or Trial Secretary for examination by owners and handlers immediately after the prizes have been awarded in each class. If score cards are distributed by a club after the prizes are awarded they must contain no more information than is shown in the judge's book and must be marked "unofficial score."

Section 8. *Announcement of Scores.* The judge shall not disclose any score or partial score to contestants or spectators until he has completed the judging of the entire class or, in case of a split class, until he has completed the judging of his division; nor shall he permit anyone else to do so. After all the scores are recorded for the class, or for the division in case of a split class, the judge shall call for all available dogs that have won qualifying scores to be brought into the ring. Before awarding the prizes, the judge shall inform the spectators as to the maximum number of points for a perfect score, and shall then announce the score of each prize winner, and announce to the handler the score of each dog that has won a qualifying score.

Section 9. *Explanations and Errors.* The judge is not required to explain his scoring, and should not enter into any discussion with any contestant who appears to be dissatisfied. Any interested person who thinks that there may have been an arithmetical error or an error in identifying a dog may report the facts to one of the stewards or to the Superintendent or Show or Trial Secretary so that the matter may be checked.

Section 10. *Rejudging.* If a dog has failed in a particular part of an exercise, it shall not ordinarily be rejudged nor given a second chance; but if in the judge's opinion the dog's preformance was prejudiced by peculiar and unusual conditions, the judge may at his own discretion rejudge the dog on the entire exercise.

Section 11. *Ties.* In case of a tie for any prize in a class, the dogs shall be tested again by having them perform at the same time all or some part of one or more of the regular exercises in that class. In the Utility class the dogs shall perform at the same time all or some part of the Signal exercise. The original scores shall not be changed.

Section 12. *Judge's Directions.* The judge's orders and signals should be given to the handlers in a clear and understandable manner, but in such a way that the work of the dog is not disturbed. Before starting each exercise, the judge shall ask "Are you ready?"

At the end of each exercise the judge shall say "Exercise finished." Each contestant must be worked and judged separately except for the Long Sit, Long Down, and Group Examination exercises, and in running off a tie.

Section 13. *A and B Classes and Different Breeds.* The same methods and standards must be used for judging and scoring the A and B classes, and in judging and scoring the work of dogs of different breeds.

Section 14. *No Added Requirements.* No judge shall require any dog or handler to do anything, nor penalize a dog or handler for failing to do anything, that is not required by these regulations.

Section 15. *Additional Commands or Signals, and Interference.* If a handler gives an additional command or signal not permitted by these regulations, either when no command or signal is permitted, or simultaneously with or following a permitted command or signal, or if he uses the dog's name with a permitted signal but without a permitted command, the dog shall be scored as though it had failed completely to perform that particular part of the exercise. A judge who is aware of any assistance, interference, or attempts to control a dog from outside the ring, must act promptly to stop any such double handling or interference, and should penalize the dog or give it less than a qualifying score if in his opinion it received such aid.

Section 16. *Standard of Perfection.* The judge must carry a mental picture of the theoretically perfect performance in each exercise and score each dog and handler against this visualized standard which shall combine the utmost in willingness, enjoyment, and precision on the part of the dog, and naturalness, gentleness, and smoothness in handling. Lack of willingness or enjoyment on the part of the dog must be penalized, as must lack of precision in the dog's performance, and roughness in handling. There shall be no penalty of less than one-half point or multiple of one-half point.

Section 17. *Qualifying Performance.* A judge's certification in his judge's book of a qualifying score for any particular dog constitutes his certification to The American Kennel Club that the dog on this particular occasion has performed all of the required exercises at least in accordance with the minimum standards and that its performance on this occasion would justify the awarding of the obedience title associated with the particular class. A qualifying score must never be awarded to a dog whose performance has not met the minimum requirements, nor to a dog that shows fear or resentment, or that relieves itself at any time in an indoor ring, or that relieves itself while performing any exercise in an outdoor ring, nor to a dog whose handler disciplines or abuses it in the ring, or carries or offers food in the ring.

In deciding whether the faulty performance of a particular exercise by a particular dog warrants a qualifying score or a score that is something less than 50% of the available points, the judge shall consider whether the awarding of an obedience title would be justified if all dogs competing in the class performed the exercise in a similar manner; and must give a score of less than 50% of the available points if he decides that it would be contrary to the best interests of the sport if all dogs competing in the class performed in a similar manner on all occasions.

Section 18. *Orders and Minimum Penalties.* The orders for the exercises and the standards for judging are set forth in the following sections. The lists of faults are not intended to be complete but minimum penalties are specified for most of the more common and serious faults. There is no maximum limit on penalties. A dog which makes none of the errors listed may still fail to qualify or may be scored zero for other reasons.

Section 19. *Heel on Leash.* The orders for this exercise are "Forward," "Halt," "Right turn," "Left turn," "About turn," "Slow," "Normal," "Fast," "Figure Eight." These orders may be given in any order and may be repeated, if necessary, but the judge shall attempt to standardize the heeling pattern for all dogs in any class. The principal feature of this exercise is the ability of the dog to work as a team with its handler. A dog that is unmanageable must be scored zero. Where a handler continually tugs on the leash or adapts his pace to that of the dog, the judge must score such a dog less than 50% of the available points. Substantial deductions shall be made for additional commands or signals to Heel and for failure of dog or handler to change pace noticeably for Slow and Fast. Minor deductions shall be made for such things as poor sits, occasionally guiding the dog with the leash, heeling wide, and other imperfections in heeling. In judging this exercise the judge shall follow the handler at a discreet distance so that he may observe any signals or commands given by the handler to the dog, but without interfering with either dog or handler.

Section 20. *Stand for Examination.* The orders for this exercise are "Stand your dog and leave when ready," "Back to your dog." The principal features of this exercise are to stand in position before and during examination and to show no shyness nor resentment. A dog that sits before or during the examination or growls or snaps must be marked zero. A dog that moves away from the place where it was left before or during the examination, or a dog that shows any shyness or resentment, must receive less than 50% of the available points. Depending on the circumstances in each case, minor or substantial deductions must be made for any dog that moves its feet at any time, or that sits, or moves away after the examination is completed. The examination shall consist of touching only the dog's head, body, and hindquarters with the fingers and palm of one hand. The scoring of this exercise will not start until the handler has given the command and/or signal to Stay, except for such things as rough treatment of the dog by its handler or active resistance by the dog to its handler's attempts to make it stand, which shall be penalized substantially.

Section 21. *Heel Free.* The order and scoring for this exercise shall be the same as for Heel on Leash except that the Figure Eight is omitted in the Heel Free exercise in the Novice classes.

Section 22. *Recall.* The orders for this exercise are "Leave your dog," "Call your dog," "Finish." The principal features of this exercise are the prompt response to the handler's command or signal to Come, and the Stay from the time the handler leaves the dog until he calls it. A dog that does not come on the first command or signal must be scored zero. A dog that does not stay without extra command or signal, or that does not come close enough so that the handler could readily touch its head without moving either foot or having to stretch forward, must receive less than 50% of the points. Substantial deductions shall be made for a slow response to the Come, depending on the specific circumstances in each case; for extra commands or signals to Stay if given before the handler leaves the dog; for a dog that stands or lies down; for extra commands or signals to Finish; and for failure to Sit or Finish. Minor deductions shall be made for poor or slow Sits or Finishes, and for a dog that touches the handler on coming in or sits between his feet.

Section 23. *Long Sit and Long Down.* The orders for these exercises are "Sit your dogs" or "Down your dogs," "Leave your dogs," "Back to your dogs." The principal features of these exercises are to stay, and to remain in the sitting or down position, whichever is required by the particular exercise. A dog that at any time during the exercise moves a substantial distance away from the place where it was left, or that goes over to any other dog, must be marked zero. A dog that stays on the spot where it was left but that fails to remain in the sitting or down position, whichever is required by the particular exercise, until the handler has returned to the heel position, and a dog that repeatedly barks or whines, must receive less than 50% of the available points. A substantial deduction shall be made for any dog that moves even a minor distance away from the place where it was left or that barks or whines only once or twice. Depending on the circumstances in each case, a substantial or minor deduction shall be made for touching the dog or for forcing it into the Down position. There shall be a minor deduction for sitting after the handler is in the heel position but before the judge has said "Exercise finished," in the Down exercises. The dogs shall not be required to sit at the end of the Down exercises.

If a dog gets up and starts to roam or follows its handler, the judge shall promptly instruct the handler or one of the stewards to take the dog out of the ring or to keep it away from the other dogs. The judge should not attempt to judge the dogs or handlers on the manner in which they are made to Sit. The scoring of the Long Sit exercise will not start until after the judge has given the order "Leave your dogs," except for such general things as rough treatment of a dog by its handler or active resistance by a dog to its handler's attempt to make it Sit.

During these exercises the judge shall stand in such a position that all of the dogs are in his line of vision, and where he can see all the handlers in the ring, or leaving and returning to the ring, without having to turn around.

Section 24. *Drop on Recall.* The orders for this exercise are the same as for the Recall, except that the dog is required to drop when coming in on command or signal from its handler when ordered by the judge, and except that an additional order or signal to "Call your dog" is given by the judge after the Drop. The dog's prompt response to the handler's command or signal to Drop is a principal feature of this exercise, in addition to the prompt responses and the Stays as described under Recall above. A dog that does not stop and drop completely on a single command or signal must be scored zero. Minor or substantial deductions shall be made for a slow drop, depending on whether the dog is just short of perfection in this respect, or very slow in dropping, or somewhere between the two extremes. All other deductions as listed under Recall above shall also apply.

The judge may designate the point at which the handler is to give the command or signal to Drop by some marker placed in advance which will be clear to the handler but not obvious to the dog, or he may give the handler a signal for the Drop, but such signal must be given in such a way as not to attract the dog's attention.

If a point is designated, the dog is still to be judged on its prompt response to the handler's command or signal rather than on its proximity to the designated point.

Section 25. *Retrieve on the Flat.* The orders for this exercise are "Throw it," "Send your dog," "Take it," "Finish." The principal feature of this exercise is to retrieve promptly. Any dog that fails to go out on the first command, or a dog that fails to retrieve, shall be marked zero. A dog that goes to retrieve before the command or signal is given, or that does not return with the dumbbell sufficiently close so that the handler can readily take it without moving either foot or stretching forward, must receive less than 50% of the points. Depending on the specific circumstances in each case, minor or substantial deductions shall be made for slowness in going out or returning or in picking up the dumbbell, mouthing or playing with the dumbbell, dropping the dumbbell, slowness in releasing the dumbbell to the handler, touching the handler on coming in, sitting between the handler's feet, failure to sit in front or to Finish. Minor deductions shall be made for poor or slow Sits or Finishes.

Section 26. *Retrieve over High Jump.* The orders for this exercise are "Throw it," "Send your dog," "Take it," and "Finish." The principal features of this exercise are that the dog must go out over the jump, pick up the dumbbell, and promptly return with it over the jump. The minimum penalties shall be the same as for the Retrieve on the Flat, and in addition a dog that fails both going and returning to go over the High Jump must be marked zero. A dog that retrieves properly but goes over the High Jump in only one direction must receive less than 50% of the available points. Substantial deductions must be made for a dog that climbs the jump or uses the top of the jump for aid in going over, in contrast to a dog that merely touches the jump. Minor deductions shall be made for touching the jump in going over.

The jumps may be preset by the stewards, based on the handler's advice as to the dog's height. The judge must make certain that the jump is set at the required height for each dog. He shall verify in the ring with an ordinary folding rule or steel tape to the nearest one-half inch, the height at the withers of each dog that jumps less than thirty-six inches. He shall not base his decision as to the height of the jump on the handler's advice.

Section 27. *Broad Jump.* The orders for this exercise are "Leave your dog," "Send your dog," and "Finish." Any dog that refuses the jump on the first command or signal or walks over any part of the jump must be marked zero. A dog that fails to stay until the handler gives the command or signal to jump, or that fails to clear the full distance with its forelegs, shall receive less than 50% of the available points. All other penalties as listed under Recall shall also apply. It is the judge's responsibility to see that the distance jumped is that required by these regulations for the particular dog.

Section 28. *Scent Discrimination.* The orders for each of these two exercises are "Send your dog," "Take it," and "Finish." The principal features of these exercises are the selection of the handler's article from among the other articles by scent alone, and the prompt carrying of the right article to the handler after its selection. The minimum penalties shall be the same as for the Retrieve on the Flat, and in addition a dog that fails to go out to the group of articles, or that retrieves a wrong article, or that fails to bring the right article to the handler must be marked zero for the particular exercise. Substantial deductions shall be made for a dog that picks up a wrong article, even though it puts it down again immediately, and for any roughness by the handler in imparting his scent to the dog. Minor or substantial deductions, depending on the circumstances in each case, shall be made for a dog that is slow or inattentive, or that does not work continuously. There shall be no penalty for a dog that takes a reasonably long time examining the articles, provided it is working smartly and continuously.

The judge shall select one article from each of the two sets and shall make written notes of the numbers of the two articles selected. The handler has the option as to which article he picks up first, but must give up each article immediately when ordered by the judge. The judge must see to it that the handler imparts his scent to the article only with his hands and that, between the time the handler picks up each article and the time he gives it to the judge, the article is held continuously in the handler's hands which must remain in plain sight. The judge or his steward must handle each of the eight other articles as he places them in the ring. The judge must make sure that they are properly separated before the dog is sent so that there may be no confusion of scent between articles.

Section 29. *Directed Retrieve*. The orders for this exercise are "Right" or "Center" or "Left," "Take it," and "Finish." The principal features of this exercise are that the dog stay until directed to retrieve, that it go directly to the designated glove, and that it retrieve promptly. A dog that fails to go out on command, or that fails to go directly in a straight line to the glove designated, or that fails to retrieve the glove shall be marked zero. A dog that goes to retrieve before the command is given, or that does not return promptly with the glove sufficiently close so that the handler can readily take it without moving either foot or stretching forward, must receive less than 50% of the available points. Depending on the specific circumstances in each case, minor or substantial deductions shall be made for touching the dog or for excessive movements in getting it to pivot at heel facing the designated glove. All of the other penalties as listed under Retrieve on the Flat shall also apply.

Section 30. *Signal Exercise*. The orders for this exercise are "Forward," "Left turn," "Right turn," "About turn," "Halt," "Slow," "Normal," "Fast," "Stand," and "Leave your dog," and in addition the judge must give the handler signals to signal his dog to Drop, to Sit, to Come, to Finish. The orders for those parts of the exercise which are done with the dog at heel may be given in any order and may be repeated if necessary, except that the order to "Stand" shall be given when the dog and handler are walking at a normal pace. The signals given the handler after he has left his dog in the Stand position shall be given in the order specified above. The principal features of this exercise are the heeling of the dog and the Come on signal as described for the Heel and Recall exercises, and the prompt response to the signals to Drop, to Sit, and to Come. A dog that fails, on a single signal from the handler, to stand or remain standing where left, or to drop, or to sit and stay, or to come, or that receives a command or audible signal from the handler to do any of these parts of the exercise, shall receive less than 50% of the available points. All of the deductions listed under the Heel and Recall exercises shall also apply to this exercise.

Section 31. *Directed Jumping.* The judge's first order is "Send your dog," then, after the dog has stopped at the far end of the ring, the judge shall designate which jump is to be taken by the dog, whereupon the handler commands and/or signals his dog to return to him over the designated jump, the dog sitting in front of the handler and finishing as in the Recall. After the dog returns to the handler the order "Finish" is given followed by "Exercise finished." The same sequence is then followed for the other jump. The principal features of this exercise are that the dog goes away from the handler in the direction indicated, stops when commanded, jumps as directed, and returns as in the Recall.

A dog that, in either half of the exercise, anticipates the handler's command and/or signal to go out, that does not leave its handler, that does not go out between the jumps and substantial distance beyond, that does not stop on command, that anticipates the handler's command and/or signal to jump, that does not jump as directed, or a dog that knocks the bar off the uprights or climbs over the High Jump or uses the top of the High Jump for aid in going over, must receive less than 50% of the available points. Substantial deductions shall be made for a dog that does not stop in the approximate center of the ring, that turns, stops, or sits, before the command to Sit, or that fails to sit. Substantial or minor deductions shall be made for slowness in going out, and all of the minimum penalties as listed under Recall shall also apply.

The judge must make certain that the jumps are set at the required height for each dog by following the same procedure described for the Retrieve over High Jump.

Section 32. *Group Examination.* The orders for this exercise are "Stand your dogs," "Leave your dogs," and "Back to your dogs." The principal features of this exercise are that the dog must stand and stay, and must show no shyness or resentment. A dog that moves a substantial distance away from the place where it was left, or that goes over to any other dog, or that sits or lies down before the handler returns to the heel position, or that growls or snaps at any time, must be marked zero. A dog that remains standing but that moves a minor distance away from the place where it was left, or a dog that shows any shyness or resentment or that repeatedly barks or whines, must receive less than 50% of the available points. Depending on the specific circumstances in each case, minor or substantial deductions must be made for any dog that moves its feet at any time during the exercise, or sits or lies down after the handler has returned to the heel position. The judge should not attempt to judge the dogs or handlers on the manner in which the dogs are made to stand. The scoring will not start until after the judge has given the order "Leave your dogs," except for such general things as rough treatment of a dog by its handler, or active resistance by a dog to its handler's attempts to make it stand. The dogs are not required to sit at the end of this exercise. The examination shall be conducted as in dog show judging, the judge going over each dog carefully with his hands. The judge must make a written record of any deductions immediately after examining each dog, subject to further deduction of points for subsequent faults. The judge must instruct one or more stewards to watch the other dogs while he conducts the individual examinations, and to call any faults to his attention.

Section 33.   *Tracking Tests.* For obvious reasons these tests cannot be held at a dog show, and a person, though he may be qualified to judge obedience trials, is not necessarily capable of judging a tracking test. He must be familiar with the various conditions that may exist when a dog is required to work a scent trail. Scent conditions, weather, lay of the land, ground cover, and wind must be taken into consideration, and a thorough knowledge of this work is necessary.

One or both of the judges must personally lay out or walk over each track after it has been laid out, a day or so before the test, so as to be completely familiar with the location of the track, landmarks, and ground conditions. At least two of the right-angle turns shall be well out in the open where there are no fences or other boundaries to guide the dog. No part of any track shall follow along any fence or boundary within fifteen yards of such boundary. The track shall include at least two right-angle turns and should include more than two such turns so that the dog may be observed working in different wind directions. Acute-angle turns should be avoided whenever possible. No conflicting tracks shall be laid. No track shall cross any body of water. No part of any track shall be laid within 75 yards of any other track. In the case of two tracks going in opposite directions, however, the first flags of these tracks may be as close as 50 yards from each other. The judges shall make sure that the track is no less than 440 yards and that the tracklayer is a stranger to the dog in each case. It is the judges' responsibility to instruct the tracklayer to insure that each track is properly laid and that each tracklayer carries a copy of the chart with him in laying the track. The judges must approve the article to be left at the end of each track, must make sure that it is thoroughly impregnated with the tracklayer's scent, and must see that the tracklayer's shoes meet the requirements of these regulations.

There is no time limit provided the dog is working, but a dog that is off the track and is clearly not working should not be given any minimum time, but should be marked Failed. The handler may not be given any assistance by the judges or anyone else. If a dog is not trailing, it shall not be marked Passed even though it may have found the article. In case of unforeseen circumstances, the judges may in rare cases, at their own discretion, give a handler and his dog a second chance on a new track. A track for each dog entered shall be plotted on the ground not less than one day before the test, the track being marked by flags which the tracklayer can follow readily on the day of the test. A chart of each track shall be made up in duplicate, showing the approximate length in yards of each leg, and major landmarks and boundaries, if any. Both of these charts shall be marked at the time the dog is tracking, one by each of the judges, so as to show the approximate course followed by the dog. The judges shall sign their charts and show on each whether the dog "Passed" or "Failed," the time the tracklayer started, the time the dog started and finished tracking, a brief description of ground, wind and weather conditions, the wind direction, and a note of any steep hills or valleys.

Melvin Powers
SELF-IMPROVEMENT
LIBRARY

Melvin Powers
SELF-IMPROVEMENT
LIBRARY

_____ CHESS STRATEGY — An Expert's Guide *Fred Reinfeld* 2.00
_____ CHESS TACTICS FOR BEGINNERS *edited by Fred Reinfeld* 2.00
_____ CHESS THEORY & PRACTICE *Morry & Mitchell* 2.00
_____ HOW TO WIN AT CHECKERS *Fred Reinfeld* 2.00
_____ 1001 BRILLIANT WAYS TO CHECKMATE *Fred Reinfeld* 2.00
_____ 1001 WINNING CHESS SACRIFICES & COMBINATIONS *Fred Reinfeld* 3.00
_____ SOVIET CHESS *Edited by R. G. Wade* 3.00

COOKERY & HERBS

_____ CULPEPER'S HERBAL REMEDIES *Dr. Nicholas Culpeper* 2.00
_____ FAST GOURMET COOKBOOK *Poppy Cannon* 2.50
_____ HEALING POWER OF HERBS *May Bethel* 2.00
_____ HERB HANDBOOK *Dawn MacLeod* 2.00
_____ HERBS FOR COOKING AND HEALING *Dr. Donald Law* 2.00
_____ HERBS FOR HEALTH How to Grow & Use Them *Louise Evans Doole* 2.00
_____ HOME GARDEN COOKBOOK Delicious Natural Food Recipes *Ken Kraft* 3.00
_____ MEDICAL HERBALIST *edited by Dr. J. R. Yemm* 3.00
_____ NATURAL FOOD COOKBOOK *Dr. Harry C. Bond* 2.00
_____ NATURE'S MEDICINES *Richard Lucas* 2.00
_____ VEGETABLE GARDENING FOR BEGINNERS *Hugh Wiberg* 2.00
_____ VEGETABLES FOR TODAY'S GARDENS *R. Milton Carleton* 2.00
_____ VEGETARIAN COOKERY *Janet Walker* 2.00
_____ VEGETARIAN COOKING MADE EASY & DELECTABLE *Veronica Vezza* 2.00
_____ VEGETARIAN DELIGHTS — A Happy Cookbook for Health *K. R. Mehta* 2.00
_____ VEGETARIAN GOURMET COOKBOOK *Joyce McKinnel* 2.00

HEALTH

_____ DR. LINDNER'S SPECIAL WEIGHT CONTROL METHOD 1.00
_____ HELP YOURSELF TO BETTER SIGHT *Margaret Darst Corbett* 2.00
_____ HOW TO IMPROVE YOUR VISION *Dr. Robert A. Kraskin* 2.00
_____ HOW YOU CAN STOP SMOKING PERMANENTLY *Ernest Caldwell* 2.00
_____ LSD — THE AGE OF MIND *Bernard Roseman* 2.00
_____ MIND OVER PLATTER *Peter G. Lindner, M.D.* 2.00
_____ NEW CARBOHYDRATE DIET COUNTER *Patti Lopez-Pereira* 1.00
_____ PSYCHEDELIC ECSTASY *William Marshall & Gilbert W. Taylor* 2.00
_____ YOU CAN LEARN TO RELAX *Dr. Samuel Gutwirth* 2.00
_____ YOUR ALLERGY—What To Do About It *Allan Knight, M.D.* 2.00

HOBBIES

_____ BEACHCOMBING FOR BEGINNERS *Norman Hickin* 2.00
_____ BLACKSTONE'S MODERN CARD TRICKS *Harry Blackstone* 2.00
_____ BLACKSTONE'S SECRETS OF MAGIC *Harry Blackstone* 2.00
_____ COIN COLLECTING FOR BEGINNERS *Burton Hobson & Fred Reinfeld* 2.00
_____ ENTERTAINING WITH ESP *Tony 'Doc' Shiels* 2.00
_____ 400 FASCINATING MAGIC TRICKS YOU CAN DO *Howard Thurston* 3.00
_____ GOULD'S GOLD & SILVER GUIDE TO COINS *Maurice Gould* 2.00
_____ HOW I TURN JUNK INTO FUN AND PROFIT *Sari* 3.00
_____ HOW TO WRITE A HIT SONG & SELL IT *Tommy Boyce* 7.00
_____ JUGGLING MADE EASY *Rudolf Dittrich* 2.00

MAGIC MADE EASY *Byron Wels*	2.00
SEW SIMPLY, SEW RIGHT *Mini Rhea & F. Leighton*	2.00
STAMP COLLECTING FOR BEGINNERS *Burton Hobson*	2.00
STAMP COLLECTING FOR FUN & PROFIT *Frank Cetin*	2.00

HORSE PLAYERS' WINNING GUIDES

BETTING HORSES TO WIN *Les Conklin*	2.00
HOW TO PICK WINNING HORSES *Bob McKnight*	2.00
HOW TO WIN AT THE RACES *Sam (The Genius) Lewin*	2.00
HOW YOU CAN BEAT THE RACES *Jack Kavanagh*	2.00
MAKING MONEY AT THE RACES *David Barr*	2.00
PAYDAY AT THE RACES *Les Conklin*	2.00
SMART HANDICAPPING MADE EASY *William Bauman*	2.00

HUMOR

BILL BALLANCE HANDBOOK OF NIFTY MOVES *Bill Ballance*	3.00
HOW TO BE A COMEDIAN FOR FUN & PROFIT *King & Laufer*	2.00

HYPNOTISM

ADVANCED TECHNIQUES OF HYPNOSIS *Melvin Powers*	1.00
CHILDBIRTH WITH HYPNOSIS *William S. Kroger, M.D.*	2.00
HOW TO SOLVE YOUR SEX PROBLEMS WITH SELF-HYPNOSIS *Frank S. Caprio, M.D.*	2.00
HOW TO STOP SMOKING THRU SELF-HYPNOSIS *Leslie M. LeCron*	2.00
HOW TO USE AUTO-SUGGESTION EFFECTIVELY *John Duckworth*	2.00
HOW YOU CAN BOWL BETTER USING SELF-HYPNOSIS *Jack Heise*	2.00
HOW YOU CAN PLAY BETTER GOLF USING SELF-HYPNOSIS *Heise*	2.00
HYPNOSIS AND SELF-HYPNOSIS *Bernard Hollander, M.D.*	2.00
HYPNOTISM *(Originally published in 1893) Carl Sextus*	3.00
HYPNOTISM & PSYCHIC PHENOMENA *Simeon Edmunds*	2.00
HYPNOTISM MADE EASY *Dr. Ralph Winn*	2.00
HYPNOTISM MADE PRACTICAL *Louis Orton*	2.00
HYPNOTISM REVEALED *Melvin Powers*	1.00
HYPNOTISM TODAY *Leslie LeCron & Jean Bordeaux, Ph.D.*	2.00
MODERN HYPNOSIS *Lesley Kuhn & Salvatore Russo, Ph.D.*	3.00
NEW CONCEPTS OF HYPNOSIS *Bernard C. Gindes, M.D.*	3.00
POST-HYPNOTIC INSTRUCTIONS *Arnold Furst*	2.00
How to give post-hypnotic suggestions for therapeutic purposes.	
PRACTICAL GUIDE TO SELF-HYPNOSIS *Melvin Powers*	2.00
PRACTICAL HYPNOTISM *Philip Magonet, M.D.*	2.00
SECRETS OF HYPNOTISM *S. J. Van Pelt, M.D.*	3.00
SELF-HYPNOSIS *Paul Adams*	2.00
SELF-HYPNOSIS Its Theory, Technique & Application *Melvin Powers*	2.00
SELF-HYPNOSIS A Conditioned-Response Technique *Laurance Sparks*	3.00
THERAPY THROUGH HYPNOSIS *edited by Raphael H. Rhodes*	3.00

JUDAICA

HOW TO LIVE A RICHER & FULLER LIFE *Rabbi Edgar F. Magnin*	2.00
MODERN ISRAEL *Lily Edelman*	2.00
OUR JEWISH HERITAGE *Rabbi Alfred Wolf & Joseph Gaer*	2.00
ROMANCE OF HASSIDISM *Jacob S. Minkin*	2.50
SERVICE OF THE HEART *Evelyn Garfield, Ph.D.*	3.00
STORY OF ISRAEL IN COINS *Jean & Maurice Gould*	2.00
STORY OF ISRAEL IN STAMPS *Maxim & Gabriel Shamir*	1.00
TONGUE OF THE PROPHETS *Robert St. John*	3.00
TREASURY OF COMFORT *edited by Rabbi Sidney Greenberg*	3.00

MARRIAGE, SEX & PARENTHOOD

ABILITY TO LOVE *Dr. Allan Fromme*	3.00
ENCYCLOPEDIA OF MODERN SEX & LOVE TECHNIQUES *Macandrew*	3.00
GUIDE TO SUCCESSFUL MARRIAGE *Drs. Albert Ellis & Robert Harper*	3.00
HOW TO RAISE AN EMOTIONALLY HEALTHY, HAPPY CHILD, *A. Ellis*	2.00
IMPOTENCE & FRIGIDITY *Edwin W. Hirsch, M.D.*	2.00
NEW APPROACHES TO SEX IN MARRIAGE *John E. Eichenlaub, M.D.*	2.00

_____SEX WITHOUT GUILT _Albert Ellis, Ph.D._		2.00
_____SEXUALLY ADEQUATE FEMALE _Frank S. Caprio, M.D._		2.00
_____SEXUALLY ADEQUATE MALE _Frank S. Caprio, M.D._		2.00
_____YOUR FIRST YEAR OF MARRIAGE _Dr. Tom McGinnis_		2.00

METAPHYSICS & OCCULT

_____BOOK OF TALISMANS, AMULETS & ZODIACAL GEMS _William Pavitt_   3.00
_____CONCENTRATION—A Guide to Mental Mastery _Mouni Sadhu_   3.00
_____DREAMS & OMENS REVEALED _Fred Gettings_   2.00
_____EXTRASENSORY PERCEPTION _Simeon Edmunds_   2.00
_____FORTUNE TELLING WITH CARDS _P. Foli_   2.00
_____HANDWRITING ANALYSIS MADE EASY _John Marley_   2.00
_____HANDWRITING TELLS _Nadya Olyanova_   3.00
_____HOW TO UNDERSTAND YOUR DREAMS _Geoffrey A. Dudley_   2.00
_____ILLUSTRATED YOGA _William Zorn_   2.00
_____IN DAYS OF GREAT PEACE _Mouni Sadhu_   2.00
_____KING SOLOMON'S TEMPLE IN THE MASONIC TRADITION _Alex Horne_ 5.00
_____MAGICIAN — His training and work _W. E. Butler_   2.00
_____MEDITATION _Mouni Sadhu_   3.00
_____MODERN NUMEROLOGY _Morris C. Goodman_   2.00
_____NUMEROLOGY—ITS FACTS AND SECRETS _Ariel Yvon Taylor_   2.00
_____PALMISTRY MADE EASY _Fred Gettings_   2.00
_____PALMISTRY MADE PRACTICAL _Elizabeth Daniels Squire_   3.00
_____PALMISTRY SECRETS REVEALED _Henry Frith_   2.00
_____PRACTICAL YOGA _Ernest Wood_   3.00
_____PROPHECY IN OUR TIME _Martin Ebon_   2.50
_____PSYCHOLOGY OF HANDWRITING _Nadya Olyanova_   2.00
_____SEEING INTO THE FUTURE _Harvey Day_   2.00
_____SUPERSTITION — Are you superstitious? _Eric Maple_   2.00
_____TAROT _Mouni Sadhu_   4.00
_____TAROT OF THE BOHEMIANS _Papus_   3.00
_____TEST YOUR ESP _Martin Ebon_   2.00
_____WAYS TO SELF-REALIZATION _Mouni Sadhu_   2.00
_____WITCHCRAFT, MAGIC & OCCULTISM—A Fascinating History _W. B. Crow_ 3.00
_____WITCHCRAFT — THE SIXTH SENSE _Justine Glass_   2.00
_____WORLD OF PSYCHIC RESEARCH _Hereward Carrington_   2.00
_____YOU CAN ANALYZE HANDWRITING _Robert Holder_   2.00

SELF-HELP & INSPIRATIONAL

_____CYBERNETICS WITHIN US _Y. Saparina_   3.00
_____DAILY POWER FOR JOYFUL LIVING _Dr. Donald Curtis_   2.00
_____DOCTOR PSYCHO-CYBERNETICS _Maxwell Maltz, M.D._   3.00
_____DYNAMIC THINKING _Melvin Powers_   1.00
_____GREATEST POWER IN THE UNIVERSE _U. S. Andersen_   4.00
_____GROW RICH WHILE YOU SLEEP _Ben Sweetland_   2.00
_____GROWTH THROUGH REASON _Albert Ellis, Ph.D._   3.00
_____GUIDE TO DEVELOPING YOUR POTENTIAL _Herbert A. Otto, Ph.D._   3.00
_____GUIDE TO LIVING IN BALANCE _Frank S. Caprio, M.D._   2.00
_____GUIDE TO RATIONAL LIVING _Albert Ellis, Ph.D. & R. Harper, Ph.D._   3.00
_____HELPING YOURSELF WITH APPLIED PSYCHOLOGY _R. Henderson_   2.00
_____HELPING YOURSELF WITH PSYCHIATRY _Frank S. Caprio, M.D._   2.00
_____HOW TO ATTRACT GOOD LUCK _A. H. Z. Carr_   2.00
_____HOW TO CONTROL YOUR DESTINY _Norvell_   2.00
_____HOW TO DEVELOP A WINNING PERSONALITY _Martin Panzer_   3.00
_____HOW TO DEVELOP AN EXCEPTIONAL MEMORY _Young & Gibson_   3.00
_____HOW TO OVERCOME YOUR FEARS _M. P. Leahy, M.D._   2.00
_____HOW YOU CAN HAVE CONFIDENCE AND POWER _Les Giblin_   2.00
_____HUMAN PROBLEMS & HOW TO SOLVE THEM _Dr. Donald Curtis_   2.00
_____I CAN _Ben Sweetland_   3.00
_____I WILL _Ben Sweetland_   2.00
_____LEFT-HANDED PEOPLE _Michael Barsley_   3.00
_____MAGIC IN YOUR MIND _U. S. Andersen_   3.00

The books listed above can be obtained from your book dealer or directly from Melvin Powers. When ordering, please remit 25c per book postage & handling. Send 25c for our illustrated catalog of self-improvement books.

Melvin Powers

12015 Sherman Road, No. Hollywood, California 91605